The OFFICIAL
ROCKY HORROR
PICTURE SHOW
AUDIENCE
PAR-TIC-I-PATION
GUIDE

by SAL PIRO
and MICHAEL HESS

Binary
PUBLICATIONS

THE ROCKY HORROR
AUDIENCE PARTICIPATION GUIDE
and COLLECTORS INDEX

This edition is a reproduction of the original book released in 1991.

Originally published by Stabur Press Inc. 1991

Current Edition
Published by Binary Publications
www.binarypubications.com

(c) 2012 Sal Piro and Michael Hess

New Collector's Guide (C) 2015 Jim Hetzer

INTRODUCTION

The Rocky Horror Picture Show is a one-of-a-kind movie. What makes this film so special is that its fans are not just passive viewers but rather they are active participants. They dress as the characters, use the props of the film, talk back to the screen and some even perform all the actions simultaneously while the movie is playing. It is this love and devotion to The Rocky Horror Picture Show that has made it the most successful midnight movie of all time.

This book is a guide to audience participation. It is not meant to be the "final word" on what to do in the theaters – but rather suggestions and ideas for "virgins" and newly-converted followers. Many of these audience "callbacks" have changed or been updated over the years. (e.g. When the Transylvanians are leaning over the lab railing, the line was "It's the King family in drag," then it changed to "It's the B-52's," then it was "We are the world," and in some places it's back to "It's the B-52's".) Some of these callbacks may be different than those that are used in your theater or area. Part of the fun of The Rocky Horror Picture Show is making up your own. Also included is a prop list, Time Warp instructions and rules of Rocky etiquette I developed many years ago. (The rules of prop use may vary according to local theater policy – so always check first.) In the back of the book, there is a special collector's guide that was developed and researched by one of Rocky Horror's biggest fans – Mike Hess.

So we hope you enjoy this guide with absolute pleasure.

Keep Time Warping,

Sal Piro

This book is dedicated to all the fans
who have made the Rocky Horror
experience so special.

Special thanks to Kim Giacchini
&
"Mad Man" Mike Ellenbogen

Official RHPS Prop List

Here is a basic list of props and instructions for their use in participation to RHPS. This list may vary according to theater policy or local customs.

1) Rice – At the beginning of the film is the wedding of Ralph Hapschatt and Betty Munroe. As the newlyweds exit the church, you should throw the rice along with the on-screen wedding guests.

2) Newspapers – When Brad and Janet are caught in the storm, Janet covers her head with a newspaper (The "Plain Dealer"). At this point, you should likewise cover your head.

3) Water pistols – These are used by members of the audience to simulate the rainstorm that Brad and Janet are caught in. (Now do you see why you should use the newspapers?)

4) Candles, flashlights – During the "There's a light" verse of "Over at the Frankenstein Place," you should light up the theater with candles, flashlights, lighters, etc. (Be careful to respect the theater's policy about open flames – remember you are wearing newspapers on your head!)

5) Rubber gloves – During and after the creation speech, Frank snaps his rubber gloves three times. Later, Magenta pulls these gloves off his hands. You should snap your gloves in sync each time to create a fantastic sound effect.

6) Noisemakers – At the end of the creation speech, the Transylvanians respond with applause and noisemakers. You should do the same.

7) Confetti – At the end of the "Charles Atlas Song" reprise, the Transylvanians throw confetti as Rocky and Frank head toward the bedroom. You should do the same.

8) Toilet paper – When Dr. Scott enters the lab, Brad cries out "Great Scott!" At this point, you should hurl rolls of toilet paper into the air. (Preferably Scotts.)

9) Toast – When Frank proposes a toast at dinner, members of the audience throw toast into the air. (Preferably unbuttered – things could get sticky.)

10) Party hat – At the diner table, when Frank puts on a party hat, you should do the same.

11) Bell – During the song "Planet Schmanet," ring the bell when Frank sings "Did you hear a bell ring?"

12) Cards – During the song "I'm Going Home" Frank sings "Cards for sorrow, cards for pain". At this point you should shower the theater with cards.

13) Hot dogs and prunes – It has happened on occasion, that fans will throw hot dogs and prunes at their appropriate mention in the film. This should not be encouraged because it attracts rodents and leaves stains on the screen.

"ROCKY HORROR" Etiquette

The difference between a true RHPS fan and someone just out for a rowdy time can be seen in their manners and etiquette. Here are some guidelines that should be deemed necessary by anyone looking to perpetuate our experiences of absolute pleasure.

1) The throwing of rice, toilet paper, water, etc. is part of the fun. It is not meant to harm people, ruin someone's make-up or costume, or cause damage to the theater.

2) Never make fun of someone for "dressing up" – especially if their costume or make-up is not exact. The point is that their heart is in it and this might discourage them or others from ever returning in costume and that's what this cult's all about, isn't it?

3) If you portray a certain character in your theater or its performing group, don't get angry or jealous if someone else comes dressed as that character. Remember that the movie and its characters are not your exclusive property. When you think about it, any resentment is hypocritical to your own "dressing up".

4) Respect the wishes of the theater and its management. Vandalism and the breaking of rules might not only lead to your ejection, but to the closing of the film. This would only be spoiling it for everyone.

5) If visitors from other theaters or areas comes to visit, don't try to "shout them down". Respect the fact that they might yell different "lines". Why, you might even find some new ones more preferable to your own.

6) Calling Brad an "asshole" and "neck lines" to the criminologist are funny in their proper place, but should not be yelled every time you see these characters' faces. It does get boring and monotonous.

AUDIENCE PARTICIPATION GUIDE

*One, Two, Three – Start the f**king movie – Four, Five, Six– forget the movie – start the f**king.*

(On screen) Twentieth Century Fox Presents
A Lou Adler/Michael White Production:

A long time ago in a galaxy far, far away, God said, 'Let there be lips.' and they were and they were good.

(LARGE PAIR OF LIPS APPEAR.)

LIPS: Michael Rennie was ill the day the earth stood still but he told us where we stand. **On our feet.** And Flash Gordon was there in silver underwear. Claude Rains was the invisible man. **Who's Claude Rains?** Then something went wrong for Fay Wray and King Kong. They got caught in a celluloid jam. **Yeah jam.** Then at a deadly pace it came from **Where?** outer space **Thank you.** and this is how the message ran.

(LIPS FREEZE- TITLE, ACTING, AND WRITING CREDITS
ROLL DURING CHORUS.)

LIPS: (Chorus)
Science Fiction – double-feature
Dr. X will build a creature.
See Androids fighting Brad and Janet.
Anne Francis stars in Forbidden Planet.
Oh – at the late night, double-feature Picture Show.

(LIPS BECOME ANIMATED AGAIN.)

LIPS: I knew Leo G. Carroll was **f**king** over a barrel when Tarantula took to the hills, **Lick it.** and I really got hot when I saw Jeannette Scott **Janet's twat** fight a triffid that spits poison and kills. **Yeah kills.** Dana Andrews said prunes gave him the runes **Shits.** and passing them used lots of skills and when worlds collide **Boom!** said George Pal to his Bride, I'm going to give you some terrible thrills. **Some joints and some pills.** Like a **Like what?**

(LIPS FREEZE AGAIN – TECHNICAL AND PRODUCTION
CREDITS ROLL DURING LAST CHORUS.)

LIPS: (Chorus)
Science Fiction - double-feature
Dr X will build a creature.
See Androids fighting Brad and Janet.
Anne Francis stars in Forbidden Planet.
Oh – at the late-night, double-feature
Picture Show
By RKO O – Oh.
At the late-night, double-feature
Picture Show.

In the back row.
*F**k the back row.*
At the late-night, double-feature
Picture Show.
I want to go
To the late night double-feature Picture Show.

(CHURCH BELLS RING - SCENE SHIFTS TO DENTON EPIS-
COPALIAN CHURCH - RALPH AND BETTY HAPSCHATT EXIT
CHURCH JUST MARRIED - FRIENDS AND FAMILY THROW
CONFETTI AND RICE.)

AUDIENCE THROWS RICE

PHOTOGRAPHER: Here they come! The parents, grandparents - yes all the close family. (Family poses for photo.) Smile! Oh, that's beautiful.

RALPH: Terrific. (Ralph approaches Brad Majors.)

BRAD: Hey Ralph.

PHOTOGRAPHER: Congratulations.

RALPH: Bye-Bye - See you.

PHOTOGRAPHER: Congratulations.

RALPH: (to Brad) Well, I guess we really did it, huh?

BRAD: I don't think there's any doubt about that - you and Betty have been almost inseparable since you met in one of Dr. Scott's refresher courses.

RALPH: Well, to tell you the truth, Brad, that was the only reason I showed up in the first place.

BETTY: OK you guys, this is it.

RALPH: Looks like Betty's gonna throw the bouquet. *Hey Janet do you have syph?*

JANET: (catches bouquet) I got it - I got it!

RALPH: Hey big fella *How would you know?* it looks like it could be your turn next, eh?

BRAD: Who knows.

RALPH: So long. See you Brad. (Ralph gets into car) *See you sucker.* Come on Betty - hop in - see you Brad. *Think about it asshole* . . . (as car drives off) *Wait til tonight, she got hers, now he'll get his.*

JANET: Oh Brad, wasn't it wonderful? Didn't Betty look radiantly beautiful?

Oh, I can't believe it. An hour ago she was plain old Betty Monroe. And now she's Mrs. Ralph Hapschatt. ***Hapshit***

BRAD: Er . . . yes, Janet . . . Ralph's a lucky guy. ***No he's not. She's got syph.***

JANET: Yes.

OLD LADY: I always cry at weddings. ***So do I, Honey.***

BRAD: Everyone knows that Betty's a wonderful little cook. ***She's the hottest baked potato in Denton . . yeah Denton! The home of happiness!***

JANET: Yes.

BRAD: Why Ralph himself will be in line for a promotion in a year or two. ***If he doesn't get busted first.***

JANET: Yes.

BRAD: Hey, Janet. ***Sit on my face and wiggle.***

JANET: Yes, Brad?

BRAD: I've got something to say. ***Say it, asshole.***

JANET: Uh-huh?

BRAD: I really love the . . . . ***Starts with an 'S'. Sku . . . Sku . . . Sku*** skillful way . . . ***What a f**king genius*** you beat the other girls . . . ***With whips and chains.*** to the bride's bouquet.

JANET: Oh Brad.

(SINGING BEGINS)

BRAD: The river was deep but I swam it.

FAMILY: Janet.

BRAD: The future is ours so let's plan it.

FAMILY: Janet.

BRAD: So please don't tell me to can it.

FAMILY: Janet.

BRAD: I've one thing to say and that's Dammit, Janet. I love you. The road was long but I ran it.

(HE RUNS BACKWARDS TOWARDS CHURCH DOORS.)

FAMILY: Janet.

BRAD: There's a fire in my heart
And you fan it.

FAMILY: Janet.

BRAD: If there's one fool for you
Then I am it.

FAMILY: Janet.

BRAD: (getting chalk from pocket) I've one thing to say and that's,
Dammit, Janet. (He chalks a heart on the church door.)
I love you. (Janet runs to him. He kneels and produces a ring.)
Here's a ring to prove that
I'm no joker.
There's three ways that love can grow that's *Gay, straight and
mediocre* good, bad or mediocre. (He drops ring and Janet picks it
up.)
Oh J-A-N-E-T *I want a blow* I love you so.

(JANET BURSTS INTO CHURCH.)

JANET: Oh! . . . . It's nicer than Betty Munroe had.

FAMILY: Oh Brad.

JANET: Now we're engaged and I'm so glad.

FAMILY: Oh Brad.

JANET: That you met Mom. And you know Dad. *F**k Mom and you blow Dad.*

FAMILY: Oh Brad.

JANET: (taking his arm) I've one thing to say. And that's,
Brad I'm mad, for you too.
Oh, Brad.

BRAD: Oh dammit. *Oh shit.*

JANET: I'm mad . . . . . .

BRAD: Oh Janet *Oh shit.*

JANET: For you.

BRAD: I love you too-oo-oo.

BRAD & JANET: There's one thing left to do-ah-ooh.

BRAD: And that's go see the man
Who began it.

FAMILY: (carrying coffin) Janet.

BRAD: When we met in his science exam
It –

FAMILY: Janet.

BRAD: Made me give you the eye
And then panic, *Piss in my pants and then panic.*

FAMILY: Janet.

BRAD: I'v got one thing to say, and that's
Dammit,
Janet.
I love you.

(JANET CIRCLES BRAD, ADMIRING HER RING ON THE
WAY.)

JANET: Oh Brad,
I'm mad. *You fag.*

BRAD: Dammit, Janet.

BRAD & JANET: I love you.

(BRAD & JANET KISS.)

(SCENE CHANGES TO THE OFFICE OF THE CRIMINOLO-
GIST. HE TURNS IN HIS ARMCHAIR AND SPEAKS DIRECTLY
TO THE AUDIENCE.)

The man you are about to see has no neck!

CRIMINOLOGIST: I would like *You would, would you.* if I may *You may.* to take
you *Where?* on a strange journey. *How strange was it? It was
so strange they made a movie about it; not the book, the movie.* It seemed a fairly ordinary night *Ordinary?* when Brad Majors *Asshole.* and his fiancee, *Slut.* Janet Weiss, *Veiss* two
young, ordinary, healthy kids, *Healthy?* left Denton that late No-
vember evening to visit a Dr. Everett Scott,

AUDIENCE BOOS & HISSES

CRIMINOLOGIST: Ex-tutor and now friend to both of them. ***Is it true that you're constipated?*** It's true . . . there were dark storm clouds, ***Describe your balls.*** heavy, black and pendulous toward which they were driving. ***Is it true that you're gay?*** It's true also that the spare tire they were carrying was badly in need of some air. ***So's your f∗∗king neck*** But they being normal kids ***Normal?*** and on a night out, well they were not going to let a storm spoil the events of their evening. ***Certainly, not.*** On a night out, ***Come a little bit closer, Chuckie.*** it was a night out they were going to remember ***For how long?*** for a very long time. ***What a f∗∗king drip.***

(SCENE SHIFTS TO A RAINY NIGHT. BRAD AND JANET ARE
DRIVING IN THEIR CAR. NIXON'S RESIGNATION SPEECH
CAN BE HEARD ON THE RADIO.)

NIXON: I have never been a quitter. ***Bullshit.*** To leave office before my term is completed is abhorrent to every instinct in my body. ***You call that a body?*** But as your President ***You call that a President?*** I must put the interests of America first. ***What does America need . . . Dick?*** America needs a full-time President ***What else?*** and a full-time congress. Particularly at this time the problems we face . . .

(A MOTORCYCLE PASSES THE CAR.)

JANET: Gosh. That's the third motorcyclist that's passed us. They certainly take their lives in their hands. What with the weather and all.

BRAD: Yes, Janet. Life's pretty cheap to that type. ***Yeah, that type.***

(THE CAR SLOWS TO A HALT.)

JANET: What's the matter Brad, darling? ***Make a sound like a cow.***

BRAD: Ooh, I think we took the wrong fork a few miles back. ***Asshole.***

JANET: Oh dear! But then where did the motorcyclists come from?

BRAD: Hmmm . . . Well, I guess we will have to turn back. ***Look Out.***

(THERE IS A NOISE FROM A TIRE EXPLODING.)

JANET: What was that bang? ***A gang bang.***

BRAD: We must have a blow-out. Dammit, I knew I should have gotten that spare tire fixed. ***Asshole.*** You just stay here and keep warm and I'll go for help.

JANET: But where will you go in the middle of nowhere? ***What's white and sells hamburgers?***

BRAD: Didn't we pass a castle down the road a few miles back? Maybe they have a telephone I could use?

JANET: I'm going with you.

BRAD: Oh, no darling, there's no sense in both of us getting wet.

JANET: I'm coming with you. *That will be a first.* Besides, darling, the owner of that phone might be a beautiful woman *He is.* and you may never come back again. *You should be so lucky.* (They both exit car into the rain.) *Kick it.*

(BRAD KICKS TIRE. JANET PUTS A NEWSPAPER ON HER HEAD TO PROTECT HER FROM RAIN.)

AUDIENCE PUTS NEWSPAPERS ON HEAD AND SPRAYS WATER PISTOLS.

(BRAD & JANET SEE GATE TO THE CASTLE WITH SIGN "ENTER AT YOUR OWN RISK" – LIGHTNING FLASHES)

Take the risk. (They Enter.) *Buy, an umbrella, you cheap Bitch!"*

JANET: (singing) In the velvet darkness of the blackest night burning bright *What's up your ass?* there's a guiding star. *That must hurt* No matter what or who you are.

BRAD & JANET: There's a light

AUDIENCE HOLDS UP LIGHTERS

VOICES: Over at the Frankenstein place

BRAD & JANET: There's a light

VOICES: Burning in the fireplace

BRAD & JANET: There's a light . . . A light in the darkness of everybody's life.

AUDIENCE PUTS OUT LIGHTERS

(RIFF RAFF APPEARS IN CASTLE WINDOW.)

"Sing to us oh hairless one."

RIFF-RAFF: (sings) The darkness must flow down the River of night's dreaming, flow, morphia slow, Let the sun and light come streaming into My life . . . into my life

BRAD & JANET: There's a light

AUDIENCE HOLDS UP LIGHTERS AGAIN.

VOICES: Over at the Frankenstein place

BRAD & JANET: There's a light

VOICES: Burning in the fireplace
there's a light, a light . . .

BRAD & JANET: In the darkness of everybody's life.

AUDIENCE PUTS OUT LIGHTERS.

(SCENE SHIFTS BACK TO CRIMINOLOGIST'S OFFICE.)

CRIMINOLOGIST: And so it seemed that fortune had smiled on Brad and Janet and that they had found the assistance that their plight required – or had they? *Nya-Hah-Hah.*

(BACK TO BRAD & JANET AT CASTLE DOOR.)

JANET: Oh, Brad, let's go back. I'm cold and I'm frightened.

BRAD: Just a moment, Janet. They may have a phone. (Brad rings doorbell.) *Ding-Dong - asshole calling.* (door opens - Riff-Raff emerges) *Say hello Riff.*

RIFF-RAFF: Hello.

BRAD: Hi. My name is Brad Majors. *Asshole.* This is my Fiancee Janet Weiss. I wonder if you might help us. You see our car broke down about two miles up the road. Do you have a phone we might use? *Look between Janet's legs.*

RIFF-RAFF: You're wet.

JANET: Yes, it's raining. *No shit Sherlock – Are you an asshole, Brad?*

BRAD: Yes. *Are you on drugs Riff*

RIFF-RAFF: Yes . . . (lightning flashes) I think perhaps you better both *Get lost.* come inside. *I don't care where you come, as long as you clean it up.*

JANET: You're too kind. (Brad & Janet follow Riff-Raff into the castle) Oh Brad, I'm frightened. What kind of place is this?

BRAD: Oh, it's probably some kind of hunting lodge for rich weirdos. *Yeah! Rich weirdos. Hey Riff, which way?*

RIFF-RAFF: This way. *Follow the bouncing thumb.*

JANET: (hearing music) Are you having a party? *No, it's my sister's Bar Mitzvah?*

RIFF-RAFF: You've arrived on a rather special night. It's one of the master's affairs. *Which one?*

JANET: Oh lucky him.

MAGENTA: (sliding down bannister) You're lucky, he's lucky, I'm lucky, we're all lucky. Ha! Ha! Ha! Ha!

(MAGENTA TOSSES FEATHER DUSTER TO RIFF-RAFF.)

Hey Riff! Show us your mother.

(RIFF OPENS GRANDFATHER CLOCK AND REVEALS SKELETON.)

RIFF-RAFF: (sings) It's astounding, time is fleeting, madness takes its toll but listen closely

MAGENTA: Not for very much longer.

RIFF RAFF: I've got to *Smoke a bowl.* keep control. I remember doing the Time Warp. *One, Two* Drinking those moments when The blackness would hit me

RIFF & MAGENTA: And the void would be calling.

(RIFF & MAGENTA LEAD BRAD & JANET INTO A BALLROOM FILLED WITH PARTY GUESTS [THE TRANSYLVANIANS].)

TRANSYLVANIANS: Let's do the Time Warp again. Let's do the Time Warp again.

(CUT TO CRIMINOLOGIST PULLING DOWN CHART WITH
DANCE INSTRUCTIONS.)

How is it done?

CRIMINOLOGIST: It's just a jump to the left

TRANSYLVANIANS: (dancing) and a step to the right . . .

CRIMINOLOGIST: With your hand on your hips

TRANSYLVANIANS: You bring your knees in tight.
But it's the pelvic thrust
That really drives you insane.
Let's do the Time Warp again.
Let's do the Time Warp again.

MAGENTA: It's so dreamy.
Oh, fantasy free me
So you can't see me
No, not at all.
In another dimension
With voyeuristic intention
Well secluded I see all.

RIFF-RAFF: With a bit of a mind flip

MAGENTA: You're into the time slip *Work that bird.*

RIFF-RAFF: And nothing can ever be the same.

MAGENTA: You're spaced out on sensation

17

RIFF-RAFF: Like you're under sedation.

TRANSYLVANIANS: Let's do the Time Warp again.
Let's do the Time Warp again.

(RIFF & MAGENTA DANCE OVER TO COLUMBIA WHO IS
SITTING ON A JUKEBOX.)

COLUMBIA: Well I was walking down the street
Just having a think
When a snake of a guy
Gave me an evil wink.
He shook me up
He took me by surprise
He had a pick-up truck
And the devil's eyes.
He stared at me
And I felt a change
Time meant nothing
Never would again.

TRANSYLVANIANS: Let's do the Time Warp again.
Let's do the Time Warp again.

CRIMINOLOGIST: It's just a jump to the left

TRANSYLVANIANS: And then a step to the right.

CRIMINOLOGIST: With your hand on your hips

TRANSYLVANIANS: You bring your knees in tight.
But it's the pelvic thrust
That really drives you insane.
Let's do the Time Warp again.
Let's do the Time Warp again.

(COLUMBIA TAP DANCES ACROSS THE BALLROOM.)

2-4-6-8-10-12-14-, eat your heart out Ann Miller.

(COLUMBIA TRIPS AND THEN JOINS RIFF AND MAGENTA
AT FRONT OF DANCE.)

CRIMINOLOGIST: It's just a jump to the left

ALL: And then a step to the right.

CRIMINOLOGIST: With your hand on your hips

ALL: You bring your knees in tight.
But it's the pelvic thrust
That really drives you insane.
Let's do the Time Warp again.
Let's do the Time Warp again.

(EVERYONE FALLS TO THE FLOOR.)

JANET: (to Brad) Say something. *Say something stupid.*

BRAD: Say, do any of you guys know how to Madison? *I do the rock myself. I do the swim.*

(BRAD & JANET BACK UP. BEHIND THEM AN ELEVATOR
SLOWLY DESCENDS.)

JANET: Brad, please let's get out of here.

Janet (SUSAN SARANDON) faints into the arms of Brad (BARRY BOSTWICK) as Riff Raff (RICHARD O'BRIEN) and Magenta (PATRICIA QUINN) dance to "The Time Warp."

BRAD: For God's sake keep a grip on yourself Janet.

JANET: But it seems so unhealthy here.

BRAD: It's just a . . . a party Janet.

JANET: Well I want to go.

BRAD: We can't go anywhere until I get to a phone.

JANET: Then ask the butler – or someone.

BRAD: Just a moment, Janet. We don't want to interfere with their celebration.

JANET: This isn't the Junior Chamber of Commerce Brad.

BRAD: They're probably foreigners with ways different from our own. – They may do some more folk dancing.

JANET: Look – I'm cold, I'm wet, and just plain scared.

BRAD: I'm here, there's nothing to worry about.

(ELEVATOR OPENS AND REVEALS DR. FRANK-N-FURTER. JANET SEES HIM. SHE SCREAMS AND FAINTS INTO BRAD'S ARMS.)

FRANK: (sings) How do you do.
I see you've met my faithful handyman.
He's a little brought down –
Because when you knocked
He thought you were the candyman.
Don't get strung out by the way that I look.
(Frank strides across the Ballroom to the throne.)
Don't judge a book by its cover
I'm not much of a man
By the light of day
But by night I'm one hell of a lover.

I'm just a Sweet Transvestite
From Transsexual Transylvania.

Let me show you around, maybe play you a sound
You look like you're both pretty groovie.
Or if you want something visual
That's not too abysmal
We could take in an old Steve Reeves movie.

BRAD: I'm glad we caught you at home.
Ah – could we use your phone?
We're both in a bit of a hurry.

JANET: Right!

BRAD: We'll just say where we are
Then go back to the car
We don't want to be any worry.

FRANK: You got caught with a flat?
Well how about that.
Well babies don't you panic.
By the light of the night
It'll all seem alright
I'll get you a satanic mechanic.

I'm just a Sweet Transvestite
From Transsexual Transylvania.

Why don't you stay for the night?

RIFF: Night.

FRANK: Or maybe a bite.

COLUMBIA: Bite.

FRANK: I could show you my favourite obsession. *Sex.*
I've been making a man *You call that a man?*
With blonde hair and a tan
And he's good for relieving my *Sexual* tension.

I'm just a Sweet Transvestite
From Transsexual Transylvania.
I'm just a Sweet Transvetite.

Frank N Furter (TIM CURRY) sings "Sweet Transvestite" with Columbia (LITTLE NELL), Magenta (PATRICIA QUINN) and Riff Raff (RICHARD O'BRIEN).

© 1975 20th Century-Fox Film Corporation. All Rights Reserved.

ALL: Sweet Transvestite.

FRANK: From Transsexual Transylvania.

GUESTS: Transylvania.

(FRANK RETURNS TO THE ELEVATOR.)

FRANK: So come up to the Lab.
And see what's on the slab *And F**k me on the slab.*
I see you shiver with antici . . . *Say it. Consta . . .*
pation.
But maybe the rain
is really to blame
so I'll remove the cause *Your clothes. But what about those nasty symptoms?*
but not the symptom.

(ELEVATOR GOES UP TO THE NEXT FLOOR.)

(RIFF & MAGENTA APPROACH BRAD & JANET AND BEGIN
TO UNDRESS THEM.)

What do you say when Brad f**ks you?

JANET: Thank you. *What do you say when Frank f**ks you?*

BRAD: Thank you very much.

JANET: Oh, Brad.

BRAD: It's alright Janet, We'll play along for now and pull out the aces when the time is right.

(RIFF & MAGENTA STRIP DOWN BRAD AND JANET TO
THEIR UNDERWEAR.)

COLUMBIA: Slowly, slowly, it's too nice a job to rush.

BRAD: Hi, my name is Brad Majors and this is my fiancee, Janet Weiss. *Veiss. Hey Brad, how do you spell urinate?* You are . . .

COLUMBIA: You are very lucky to be invited up to Frank's laboratory. Some people would give their right arm for the privilege. *Or their left tit.*

BRAD: People like you maybe?

COLUMBIA: Hah, I've seen it.

(BRAD & JANET ARE LED TO THE ELEVATOR.)

MAGENTA: Come along the Master doesn't like to be kept waiting. *What do you do to an uncomfortable c**k?* Shift It! *Drop it!*

(RIFF-RAFF DROPS BOTTLE)

Thank you.

(RIFF-RAFF CLOSES DOOR AND TAKES ELEVATOR UP TO
THE LABORATORY.)

JANET: (To Magenta) Is he, Frank I mean, is he your husband?

RIFF-RAFF: The Master is not yet married. Nor do I think he ever will be. We are simply his *Slaves.* servants.

(ELEVATOR ARRIVES AT LABORATORY. FRANK IS SEEN IN
GREEN SURGICAL GOWN. RIFF-RAFF OPENS GATE AND
MOTIONS FOR BRAD & JANET TO EXIT.)

Sluts first, assholes second, groupies and monsters third.

(AS THEY EXIT, WE SEE THE ENTIRE LAB.)

And all this can be yours if the price is right.

(THE TRANSYLVANIANS ARE ON THE LEVEL ABOVE
LEANING OVER THE RAILING.)

We are the world.
What's your favorite color?

FRANK: Magenta, *Where do you get your pot?* Columbia, go and assist Riff-Raff. *Woof-Woof.* I will entertain . . . ah . . . (Extends hand) *Reach out, reach out and touch someone.*

BRAD: Brad Majors, *Asshole.* and this is my fiancee, Janet Veiss. *Weiss.*

JANET: Weiss.

BRAD: Weiss. *Frank, do you speak French?*

FRANK: Enchanté . . . Well, how nice. And what charming underclothes you both have. But here put these on. *And take those off.* They'll make you feel less *Naked.* vulnerable. It's not often we receive visitors here. Let alone offer them hospitality. *Horse brutality.*

BRAD: Hospitality! All we wanted to do was use your telephone, Goddammit. A reasonable request which you have chosen to ignore.

JANET: Don't be ungrateful Brad.

BRAD: Ungrateful!!

FRANK: *Superman.* How forceful you are Brad. Such a perfect specimen of manhood. So dominant. *Big.* You must be awfully proud of him Janet. *Hey Janet, are you a slut?*

JANET: Well, yes I am.

FRANK: Do you have any tattoos Brad?

BRAD: Certainly not! ***Ask the bitch.***

FRANK: Oh well. How about you? (He laughs.)

RIFF-RAFF: Everything is in readiness, Master. We merely await your word. (Frank passes champagne glass to Riff-Raff.) ***No, not on my suit, I just had it cleaned.*** (Champagne spills on Riff-Raff.) ***Oh shit.***

(FRANK CROSSES TO PODIUM BETWEEN MAGENTA & COLUMBIA.)

Hey Frank, when's the orgy?

Frank N Furter (TIM CURRY) announces the creation of Rocky with Magenta (PATRICIA QUINN) and Columbia (LITTLE NELL) at his side.

FRANK: Tonight, my unconventional conventionists. You are to witness a breakthrough in biochemical research. And paradise is to be mine. (Everyone applauds.) It was strange the way it happened. Suddenly, you get a break.

(SNAPS HIS GLOVES.)

AUDIENCE SNAPS RUBBER GLOVES

FRANK: All the pieces seem to fit into place. What a sucker you've been. What a fool. The answer was there all the time. It took a small accident to make it happen. ***A what?*** An accident!!

MAGENTA & COLUMBIA: (Whisper to Frank.) An accident.

FRANK: And that's how I discovered the secret. That elusive ingredient. ***Who's your favorite on 'Star Trek'?*** That spark that is the breath of life. ***Do you know about gay sex?*** Yes, I have that knowledge. ***What do you hold under your arm?*** I hold the secret ***To life?*** to life ***Itself?*** itself!

(FRANK CROSSES TO TANK AND SNAPS GLOVES.)

AUDIENCE SNAPS GLOVES.

(TRANSYLVANIANS APPLAUD AND USE NOISEMAKERS.)

AUDIENCE USES NOISEMAKERS.

F

FRANK: You see *K* you are fortunate. For tonight is the night.

(FRANK SNAPS GLOVES.)

AUDIENCE SNAPS GLOVES.

FRANK: That my beautiful creature is destined to be born. *F**ked.*

(TRANSYLVANIANS APPLAUD AND USE NOISEMAKERS.)

AUDIENCE USES NOISEMAKERS.

(FRANK TURNS TO COVERED TANK.)

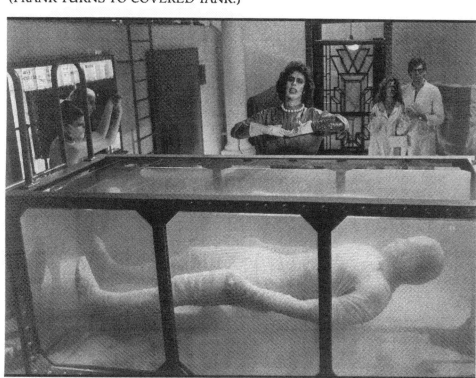

Frank N Furter (TIM CURRY) unveils his monster as Janet (SUSAN SARANDON) and Brad (BARRY BOSTWICK) watch.

FRANK: Hoopla!

(MAGENTA & COLUMBIA RAISE COVER OFF TANK. WE SEE
A FORM INSIDE THE TANK.)

FRANK: Throw open the switches on the sonic oscillator. (Riff-Raff pulls down two switches.) and step up the reactor power input three more points.

(RIFF-RAFF PRESSES THREE BUTTONS AND BEGINS TO UNWIND A WHEEL. FRANK WATCHES EXCITEDLY AS A CHANDELIER IS LOWERED.)

JANET: Oh, Brad . . .

BRAD: It's alright, Janet.

(WHEN THE CHANDELIER IS LOWERED OVER THE TANK FRANK SPURTS DIFFERENT COLORED LIQUIDS ONTO THE "FORM" IN THE TANK. THE LIQUIDS DRAIN AWAY. THE "FORM" ALL WRAPPED IN BANDAGES BEGINS TO MOVE AND STANDS UP. RIFF-RAFF REMOVES THE BANDAGE FROM ITS HEAD. THE "FORM" IS 'ROCKY HORROR'.)

FRANK: (Seeing the face.) Oh, Rocky!!

(ROCKY IS HANGING ONTO THE CHANDELIER WHICH RIFF-RAFF IS WINDING UPWARDS.)

ROCKY: (Sings) The Sword of Damocles is
Hanging over my head.

And I've got the feeling
Someone's going to be
Cutting the thread. ***Kick him.***

(FRANK KICKS RIFF-RAFF WHO LOWERS CHANDELIER.)

ROCKY: Oh, woe is me.
My life is a misery.

Oh, can't you see
That I'm at the start
Of a pretty big downer . . .

(AFTER ROCKY IS LOWERED TO THE GROUND, MAGENTA AND COLUMBIA BEGIN TO CUT AND UNWRAP HIS BANDAGES.)

ROCKY: I woke up this morning
with a start
when I fell out of bed.

TRANSYLVANIANS: That ain't no crime.

ROCKY: And left from my dreaming
Was a feeling
Of un-nameable dread.

TRANSYLVANIANS: That ain't no crime.

ROCKY: My high is low.
I'm dressed up
With no place to go.

And all I know
Is I'm at the start
Of a pretty big downer.

FRANK: Oh, Rocky!

TRANSYLVANIANS: (Including Riff-Raff, Magenta, & Columbia.)
Sha la la la
That ain't no crime.

ROCKY: Oh, no, no, no, no.

TRANSYLVANIANS: Sha la la la
That ain't no crime –
That ain't no crime.

(ROCKY IS NOW UNBANDAGED. HE STRIKES A POSE.
DURING THE LAST CHORUS, FRANK CLIMBS OUT OF THE
TANK ONTO RIFF-RAFF'S SHOULDERS AND PURSUES
ROCKY, BUT THEY FALL.)

Dr. Frank N Furter (TIM CURRY) admires his new creation, "Rocky" (PETER HINWOOD).

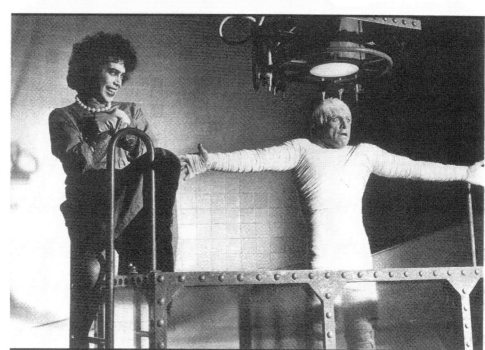

ROCKY: (To first group of Transylvanians.)
The sword of Damocles is
Hanging over my head.

TRANSYLVANIANS: That ain't no crime.

ROCKY: (To second group.)
And I've got the feeling
Someone's going to be
Cutting the thread.

TRANSYLVANIANS: That ain't no crime.

ROCKY: (To third group.)
Oh, woe is me –
My life is a mystery.

(To fourth group.)
And can't you see
That I'm at the start
Of a pretty big downer.

(FRANK IS CHASING ROCKY AROUND THE LAB.)

TRANSYLVANIANS: Sha la la la
That ain't no crime.

ROCKY: Oh no no no no.

TRANSYLVANIANS: Sha la la la
That ain't no crime.

ROCKY: No no no no.

TRANSYLVANIANS: Sha la la la
That ain't no crime –
That ain't no crime.

TRANSYLVANIANS: Sha la la la
That ain't no crime.

ROCKY: No no no no.

TRANSYLVANIANS: Sha la la la
That ain't no crime.

ROCKY: No no no no.

TRANSYLVANIANS: Sha la la la
That ain't no crime –
That ain't no crime.

(ROCKY HAS CLIMBED BACK ONTO THE TANK. FRANK
CATCHES UP TO HIM.)

FRANK: Well, really. That's no way to behave on your first day out. But since you're such an exceptional beauty I'm prepared to forgive you. Oh, I just love success.

RIFF-RAFF: He is a credit to your genius, Master.

FRANK Yes.

MAGENTA: A triumph of your vill.

FRANK: Yes.

COLUMBIA: He's o.k.

FRANK: OK? *Hey Frank, How do you kill roaches?* (Frank slams hand on tank.) OK? I think we can do better than that? *Why don't you ask Brad & Janet?* Well, Brad and Janet, *Tap-tap-tap* (Frank taps Rocky's shoulders.) what do you think of him? *Lie, Janet.*

JANET: Well, I don't like men with too many muscles. *Til later.*

FRANK: I didn't make him for you. He carries the Charles Atlas seal of approval.

(FRANK LEADS ROCKY AWAY TO GIVE HIM HIS BIRTHDAY
PRESENTS.)

FRANK: (Singing.)
A weakling weighing
Ninety eight pounds
Will get sand in his face
When kicked to the ground.
And soon in the gym
With a determined chin
The sweat from his pores
As he works for his ca-ha-hause.

Will make him glisten *What's your favorite toothpaste?*
And gleam.
And with massage and just a little bit of ste-he-he-he-heam *Go for it.* (Franks finger is slowly going down Rocky's chest to his groin. The finger falls off Rocky.) *Close – but no cigar.*
He'll be pink and quite clean.
He'll be a strong man –
Oh honey –

TRANSYLVANIANS: But the wrong man.

FRANK: He'll eat nutritious high protein
And swallow raw eggs.
Try to build up his shoulders,
His chest, arms and legs.

Such an effort –
If he only knew of my plan.
In just seven days,

TRANSYLVANIANS: I can make you a ma-aa-a-a-an.

FRANK: He'll do press-ups and chin-ups,
Do the snatch clean and jerk. *Off.*

He thinks dynamic tension
Must be hard work.
Such strenuous living
I just don't understand.

When, in just seven days –
Oh baby . . .

I can make you
A ma-a-a-a-an . . .(Laugh.)

(A LARGE REFRIGERATION UNIT OPENS LIKE A
DRAWBRIDGE.)

COLUMBIA: (Screaming.) Eddie!!

(EDDIE BREAKS THROUGH CAKES OF ICE ON HIS MOTOR-
CYCLE. HE THROWS OFF HELMET AND GETS OFF BIKE.)

EDDIE: (Singing.)
Whatever happened to Saturday night
When you dressed up sharp
And you felt alright?
It don't seem the same since cosmic light
Came into my life, I thought I was divine.

I used to go for a ride with a chick who'd go
and listen to the music on the radio.
A saxophone was blowing on a rock and roll show.
We climbed in the backseat.
We really had a good time.

Hot patootie
Bless my soul
I really love that rock and roll.

EDDIE & ALL: Hot patootie
Bless my soul
I really love that rock and roll.

Hot patootie
Bless my soul
I really love that rock and roll.

Hot patootie
Bless my soul
I really love that rock and roll.

(EDDIE PLAYS A SAXOPHONE SOLO.)

EDDIE: My head used to swim
From the perfume I smelled.

My hands kind of fumbled
With her white plastic belt.
I'd taste her baby pink lipstick,
And that's when I'd melt.
And she'd whisper in my ear,
Tonight she really was mine.

Get back in front and put
Some hair oil on.
Buddy Holly was singing
His very last song.
With your arms around your girl
You tried to – ah – sing along
If felt pretty good, whoo.
Really had a good ti-i-ime.

(EDDIE DANCES WITH COLUMBIA.)

EDDIE: Hot patootie
Bless my soul
I really love that rock and roll.

EDDIE & ALL: Hot patootie
Bless my soul
I really love that rock and roll.

Hot patootie
Bless my soul
I really love that rock and roll.

Hot patootie
Bless my soul
I really love that rock and roll.

(TRANSYLVANIANS DANCE IN A KICK LINE. FRANK GETS
UPSET. EDDIE GETS ON MOTORCYCLE AND DRIVES
AROUND THE LAB.)

EDDIE & ALL: Hot patootie
Bless my soul
I really love that rock and roll.

Hot patootie
Bless my soul
I really love that rock and roll.

Hot patootie
Bless my soul
I really love that rock and roll.

Hot patootie
Bless my soul
I really love that rock and roll.

Hot patootie
Bless my soul
I really love that rock and roll.

Hot patootie
Bless my soul
I really love that rock and roll.

Hot patootie
Bless my soul
I really love that rock and roll.

Hot patootie
Bless my soul
I really love that rock and roll.

(WHEN EDDIE PULLS UP ON BIKE, FRANK CHASES HIM
WITH AN ICE PICK INTO REFRIGERATOR. FRANK HACKS
EDDIE TO DEATH. COLUMBIA IS SCREAMING.)

FRANK: One from the vaults. *A greaser from the freezer, a bat out of hell.* (Frank extends gloves to Magenta for removal.) *What does Magenta do with bloody rubbers? She turns them inside out and uses them again.*

(ROCKY RATTLES ELEVATOR DOOR.)

FRANK: Oh, Baby! *I'm upset* Don't be upset, it was a mercy-killing. *Mercy, mercy, mercy.* He had a certain naive charm, but no muscle. *Pump it.*

FRANK: (Sings.)
But a deltoid and a bicep
A hot groin and a tricep
Makes me shake. *Dance with a midget.*
Makes me want to take Charles
Atlas by the hand. *Balls.*
In just seven days *That's a week.*
Oh, Baby

FRANK & TRANSYLVANIANS: I can make you a ma-ha-ha-ha-haan.

FRANK: I don't want no dissension
Just dynamic tension *Sing it bitch.*

JANET: I'm a muscle fan.

FRANK & TRANSYLVANIANS: In just seven days *That's a week.*
I can make you
A ma-ha-ha-ha-haan.

FRANK: Dig it, if you can.

FRANK & TRANSYLVANIANS: In just seven days *That's a week.*
I can make you
A ma-ha-ha-ha-haan.

(FRANK LEADS ROCKY TO BRIDAL SUITE.)

(TRANSYLVANIANS THROW CONFETTI.)

AUDIENCE THROWS CONFETTI

(SCENE SHIFTS BACK TO CRIMINOLOGIST'S OFFICE.)

I say that life is an illusion.

CRIMINOLOGIST: There are those who say that life is an illusion. *Like your neck.* And that reality is simply a figment of the imagination. *Like your neck.* If this is so, then Brad and Janet are quite safe. However, the sudden departure of their host and his creation into the seclusion of his somber bridal suite *Sweeeet.* had left them feeling both apprehensive and uneasy. A feeling which grew *Greeew! Unlike your neck.* as the other guests "departed" and "they" were shown to their separate rooms.

(JANET IS LED INTO PINK BEDROOM BY COLUMBIA.)

Pink is for sluts. Watch your back.

(JANET BACKS INTO WATER BASIN.)

(RIFF AND MAGENTA WATCH JANET ON TELEVISION
MONITOR.)

He sees you when you're sleeping, he knows when you're awake, he knows when you are bad or good or when you masturbate.

(BRAD IS LED INTO BLUE BEDROOM BY COLUMBIA.)

And blue is for assholes.

(CUT BACK TO RIFF & MAGENTA VIEWING JANET.)

Sit down, Bitch.

(JANET SITS ON BED.)

(LATER WHILE JANET IS IN BED, THERE IS A KNOCK AT
THE DOOR.)

JANET: Who is it? Who's there?

BRAD'S VOICE: It's only me, Janet.

JANET: Oh, Brad, darling, come in *And out and in again.* (Frank, impersonating Brad gets into bed.) Oh Brad - mmmm – Oh yes, my darling – oh, but what if . . . .

BRAD: It's alright Janet. Everything's going to be alright.

JANET: Oh, I hope so my darling . . .Oh, oh it's you!!

FRANK: I'm afraid so Janet. But isn't it nice?

JANET: You beast, you monster, what have you done with Brad?

FRANK: Nothing. *Yet.* Why, do you think I should?

JANET: You tricked me – I wouldn't have – I've never – never

FRANK: Yes, yes I know. But it wasn't all bad was it? *It isn't all Brad either.* I think you really found it quite pleasurable.

JANET: Oh – Oh – no – stop – I mean help. I – Brad – Oh. (She shouts.) Brad.

FRANK: Ssssh. Brad's probably asleep by now. Do you want him to see you like this?

JANET: Like this – like how? It's your fault. You're to blame. I was saving myself. *So was I, honey.*

FRANK: Well, I'm sure you're not spent yet. *For a nickel I will.*

JANET: Promise you won't tell Brad.

FRANK: Cross my heart and hope to die.

(JANET SQUEALS WITH EXCITEMENT.)

Stick a dildoe in my eye.

(SCENE CHANGES TO THE LAB. MAGENTA IS MOPPING
AND RIFF-RAFF APPROACHES HER.)

*(Sings.) I'm so glad we had this time together.
Hey Magenta, can I borrow your mopstick? I got the perfect
place to put it.*

(AFTER A PRIVATE DISCUSSION, RIFF APPROACHES THE
BEDROOM. ROCKY IS CHAINED TO THE BED FACE DOWN)

(Sings.) Rocky takes it up the ass, doo-dah. doo-dah.

(RIFF-RAFF PICKS UP CANDELABRA.)

*Is it the butcher? – No! Is it the baker? – No! It's the 44 candle
killer!!*

(RIFF-RAFF TAUNTS ROCKY.)

How about a little fire, scarecrow?

(ROCKY BREAKS CHAINS AND ESCAPES DOWN ELEVATOR
SHAFT.)

Can we have a light down here?

(RIFF-RAFF THROWS CANDLE DOWN SHAFT. HE PUTS
DOWN CANDELABRA AND TOUCHES ELBOWS WITH
MAGENTA.)

*On a hot summer night, would you offer your throat to the
wolf with the red roses.*

(RIFF-RAFF KISSES MAGENTA ON THE NECK.)

Incest is best.

(SCENE CHANGES TO BRAD'S BEDROOM. BRAD IS IN BED
AND FRANK IMPERSONATING JANET RUNS IN.)

Hey Brad, what time is it?

(BRAD LOOKS AT HIS WATCH.)

JANET'S VOICE: Oh Brad, darling, it's no good here. It will destroy us.

BRAD: Don't worry Janet, we'll be away from here in the morning.

JANET'S VOICE: Oh, Brad, you're so strong and protective.

(BRAD CARESSES "HER" HAIR AND FRANK'S WIG
COMES OFF.)

BRAD: You!!!

FRANK: I'm afraid so, Brad. But wasn't it nice?

BRAD: Why you – what have you done with Janet? *F**ked the shit out
of her.*

FRANK: Nothing. Why, do you think I should?

BRAD: You tricked me. I wouldn't have – I've never – never, never. *Not
even in Boy Scout camp?*

FRANK: Yes, I know, but it isn't all bad is it? Not even half bad? I think you
found it quite pleasurable.

BRAD: Ahhh – no – stop – I mean Janet, (Shouts.) Janet.

FRANK: Shush. Janet's probably asleep by now. Do you want her to see you like this?

BRAD: Like this. Like how? It's your fault – you're to blame. I thought it was the real thing. *It is!*

FRANK: Oh, come on, Brad, admit it. You liked it, didn't you? There's no crime in giving yourself over to pleasure. *It is in New Jersey.* Oh Brad, you have wasted so much time already. Janet needn't know, I won't tell her.

BRAD: Well, you promise you won't tell?

FRANK: On my mother's grave.

(RIFF-RAFF APPEARS ON A TV MONITOR.)

RIFF-RAFF: Master, Rocky has broken his chains and vanished. The new play-mate is loose and somewhere in the castle grounds. Magenta has just released the dogs. *Film at eleven.*

FRANK: Coming! *So is Brad.*

(SCENE CHANGES TO JANET'S BEDROOM.)

JANET: What's happening here? Where's Brad? Where's anybody?

(ROCKY IS SEEN BEING CHASED AROUND THE GROUNDS
BY THE DOGS.)

(JANET IS NOW IN THE ELEVATOR.)

JANET: Oh, Brad. *Oh, Janet.* Brad my darling *Janet, my fish.* How could I have done this to you? *It was easy, but it would have been easier without the panty hose.*

(ELEVATOR RISES [WE SEE HER PANTYHOSE] TO THE LAB
– JANET EXITS.)

JANET: If only we hadn't made this journey. *But you did.* If only the car hadn't broken down. *But it did.* If only we were amongst friends *But you aren't.* or sane persons. *Two out of three ain't bad.* Oh Brad, what have they done with him?.

(JANET GOES TO TELEVISION MONITOR. SHE SEES BRAD
& FRANK.)

JANET: *Yes, Janet, Brad smokes.* Oh Brad, how could you . . .

(JANET HEARS CRYING AND CROSSES OVER TO
THE TANK.)

Leave him alone, he's monsterbating.

(SHE LIFTS COVER AND ROCKY POPS UP.)

JANET: Oh, but you're hurt. ***Kiss my boo-boo.*** Did they do this to you? ***They sure did! Those snivelling shits.*** Here I'll dress your wounds. ***And undress mine.*** Baby there . . . ***That's no baby Janet.*** (Rocky touches Janet's hand.) ***Hey Janet, you wanna f**k? Think about it. Smile if you're horny, bitch.***

(JANET SMILES.)

(SCENE CHANGES TO CRIMINOLOGIST'S OFFICE. HE IS READING FROM A DICTIONARY.)

CRIMINOLOGIST: "Emotion." Agitation or disturbance of mind. Vehement or excited mental state. ***And you can only read about it, shitlips.*** It is also a powerful and irrational ***Mouthwash.*** master. And from what Magenta and Columbia eagerly viewed on their television monitor, there seemed to be little doubt that Janet was ***A nympho-maniac.*** indeed its slave.

(COLUMBIA & MAGENTA ARE LOOKING ON THEIR MONITOR.)

COLUMBIA & MAGENTA: Tell us about it, Janet. (They laugh.)

(SCENE CHANGES TO JANET AND ROCKY IN THE LAB.)

JANET: (Sings.) I was feeling done in ***And pushed up.***
Couldn't win ***Like the Mets.***
I'd only ever kissed before ***Bullshit!***

COLUMBIA: You mean she . . .?

MAGENTA: Uh-huh.

JANET: I thought there's no use getting ***Laid.***
Into heavy petting
It only leads to trouble
And seat wetting ***Yeah! Wet seats.***
Now all I want to know
Is how to go
I've tasted ***Cum.*** blood
And I want more

COLUMBIA & MAGENTA: More, More, More!

JANET: I'll put up no resistance
I want to stay the distance
I've got an itch to scratch
I need assistance

Touch-a touch-a touch me.
I wanna be dirty.
Thrill me, chill me, fulfill me.
Creature of the night.

(ROCKY BENDS DOWN BETWEEN JANETS LEGS AND
CROSSES TO OTHER SIDE OF THE TANK.)

Smells like fish. This is a good place for a stick-up.

JANET: Then if anything grows (She laughs.)
While you pose,
I'll oil you up
And rub you down

COLUMBIA & MAGENTA: Down, Down, Down!

JANET: And that's just one small fraction
Of the main attraction.
You need a friendly hand,
Oh, and I need action.

Tough-a touch-a touch-a, touch me.
I wanna be dirty.
Thrill me, chill me, fulfill me.
Creature of the night.

COLUMBIA: Touch-a touch-a touch-a touch me.

MAGENTA: I wanna be dirty.
COLUMBIA: Thrill me, chill me, fulfill me

MAGENTA: Creature of the night.

JANET: Oh, touch-a touch-a touch-a touch me.
I wanna be dirty.
Thrill me, chill me, fulfill me – oh –
Creature of the night.

Creature of the ni-i-ight.

ROCKY: Creature of the night.

BRAD: Creature of the night.

FRANK: Creature of the night.

MAGENTA: Creature of the night.

RIFF-RAFF: Creature of the night.

COLUMBIA: Creature of the night.

ROCKY: Creature of the night.

JANET: Creature of the night.

(FRANK, RIFF AND BRAD COME UP THE ELEVATOR INTO
THE LAB. FRANK IS WHIPPING RIFF-RAFF.)

Hit him, hit him again, harder.

RIFF-RAFF: Aaaargh! Mercy.

FRANK: How did it happen? I understood you were to be watching.

RIFF-RAFF: I was only away for a minute, master.

FRANK: Well, see if you can find him on the monitor. *Hey Frank, hows your backhand?*

(FRANK HITS HIM ONE MORE TIME.)

(RIFF-RAFF TURNS ON THE MONITOR. DR. SCOTT IN A WHEELCHAIR IS SEEN ON THE SCREEN.)

It's R-2 D-2.

RIFF-RAFF: Master, master, we have a visitor. *What does Captain Kirk say to his chief Engineer?*

BRAD: Hey, Scotty – Dr. Everett Scott.

RIFF-RAFF: You know this earthling *Watch it O'Brien.* . . . person?

BRAD: I most certainly do. He happens to be an old friend of mine. *What's your favorite fruit drink?*

FRANK: I see. So this wasn't simply a chance meeting. You came here with *On a porpoise.* a purpose.

BRAD: I told you, my car broke down. I was telling you the truth. *A lie.*

FRANK: I know what you told me, Brad. But this Dr. Everett Scott. His name is not unknown to me.

BRAD: He was a science teacher at Denton High School.

FRANK: And now he works for your government, doesn't he, Brad? He's attached to the Bureau of Investigation of that which you call U.F.O.'s. Isn't that right Brad?

BRAD: He might be. I don't know.

RIFF-RAFF: The intruder is entering the building, master. *Where could he be?*

FRANK: He'll probably be in the Zen room. *Not the Zen room.*

(DR. SCOTT IS SEEN IN ZEN ROOM WITH MAGNIFYING GLASS EXAMINING "CIGARETTE BUTTS".)

Smoke it! This house has roaches.

FRANK: Shall we inquire of him in person? *Oh, no, not the triple-contact-electro-magnet.*

(FRANK THROWS A SWITCH MARKED "TRIPLE CONTACT ELECTRO MAGNET. DR. SCOTT AND HIS WHEELCHAIR ARE DRAWN UP THE STAIRS. HE PASSES THROUGH MAGENTA & COLUMBIA'S ROOM.)

Next time knock.

(HE IS DRAWN UP THE NEXT FLIGHT OF STAIRS AND CRASHES THROUGH THE LABORATORY WALL.)

BRAD: Great Scott!

AUDIENCE THROWS TOILET PAPER ROLLS.

(DR. SCOTT ROLLS DOWN THE RAMP RIGHT INTO THE MAGNET.)

DR. SCOTT: Frank-N-Furter. *Mit Kraut.* We meet at last. *No, we meet at first.*

BRAD: Dr. Scott. (Extends hand.)

DR. SCOTT: Brad, what are you doing here? *Oh, just f**king around.*

FRANK: Don't play games, Dr. Scott. You know perfectly well what Brad Major's is doing here. *Getting good head.* It was part of your plan was it not, that he, and his female, should check the layout for you? *Check the lay, anyway.* Well, unfortunately for you all, the plans are to be changed. I hope you're adaptable Dr. Scott. I know Brad is. *You promised you wouldn't tell.*

DR. SCOTT: I can assure you that Brad's presence here comes as a complete surprise to me. I came here to find *Sweaty.* Eddie.

BRAD: Eddie? I've seen him. He's . . .

(FRANK CUTS IN QUICKLY.)

FRANK: Eddie? What do you know of Eddie, Dr. Scott? *Get conceited.*

DR. SCOTT: I happen to know a great deal about a lot of things. You see, Eddie happens to be my *My dinner.* nephew.

(JANET MOANS FROM TANK.)

You blew it bitch.

BRAD: Dr. Scott. *Mouseketeer roll call, sound off.*

Riff Raff (RICHARD O'BRIEN), Frank N Furter (TIM CURRY) and Magenta (PATRICIA QUINN) attend a banquet.

(FRANK CROSSES TO TANK AND PULLS OFF COVER. JANET
AND ROCKY ARE REVEALED.)

DR. SCOTT: Janet! *Janet!*

JANET: Dr. Scott! *Dr. Scott!*

BRAD: Janet! *Janet!*

JANET: Brad! *Brad!*

FRANK: Rocky! *Rocky!*

(ROCKY GLARES.)*Uhhhh!*

DR. SCOTT: Janet! *Janet!*

JANET: Dr. Scott! *Dr. Scott!*

BRAD: Janet! *Janet!*

JANET: Brad! *Brad!*

FRANK: Rocky! *Rocky!*

(ROCKY GLARES.) *Uhhhh!*

DR. SCOTT: Janet! *Janet!*

JANET: Dr. Scott! *Dr. Scott!*

BRAD: Janet! *Janet!*

JANET: Brad! *Brad!*

FRANK: Rocky! *Rocky!*

(ROCKY GLARES.) *Uhhhh!*

What do you say to a piece of shit?

FRANK: Listen! I made you and I can break you just as easily. *I'm hungry.*

(MAGENTA SOUNDS A LARGE GONG.)

MAGENTA: Master, dinner is prepared! *And we helped. What do you think of oral sex?*

FRANK: Excellent. Under the circumstances, formal dress is to be optional. *Toga! Toga! Toga!*

(SCENE CHANGES BACK TO CRIMINOLOGIST'S OFFICE.)

CRIMINOLOGIST: Food has always played a vital role in life's rituals. The breaking of bread – the last meal of the condemned man – *The munchies.* and now this meal. However informal it might appear, you can be sure there was to be very little "bonhomie". *Bon-a-who?*

(SCENE CHANGES TO DINING ROOM. FRANK, ROCKY, COLUMBIA, BRAD, JANET AND DR. SCOTT ARE SEATED AT DINNER TABLE. RIFF AND MAGENTA ROLL IN SERVING CART. THEY DROP A JOINT OF MEAT ON FRANK'S PLATE.)

Not meatloaf again?

(MAGENTA HANDS FRANK AN ELECTRIC CARVING KNIFE.)

Always reach for a Hamilton-Beach. Gentlemen, start your engines.

(FRANK SLICES MEAT. RIFF & MAGENTA START SERVING WINE. ROCKY STARTS TO DRINK. FRANK POINTS KNIFE AT HIM.)

Wait for the toast.

(ROCKY PUTS GLASS DOWN.)

Wow, I could have had a V-8.

(RIFF SPILLS WINE ON DR. SCOTT'S PLATE.)

(DR. SCOTT PUTS NAPKIN ON HIS LAP. FRANK FINISHES
AND RAISES HIS GLASS.)

FRANK: A toast . . . *To cannibalism.*

AUDIENCE THROWS TOAST.

FRANK: . . . to absent friends.

AUDIENCE CAN NAME FRIENDS NOT THERE.

. . . and Rocky.

AUDIENCE HUMS 'ROCKY' THEME.

AUDIENCE PUTS ON BIRTHDAY HATS.

FRANK: (Sings.) Happy Birthday to you. *Wooo*

EVERYONE: Happy Birthday to you. *Wooo*
Happy Birthday dear Rocky.

FRANK: Shall we.

(RIFF-RAFF TOSSES SLICES OF MEAT ONTO THEIR PLATES.)

Hey Riff, deal me a slice.

(COLUMBIA NUDGES ROCKY TO USE FORK.)

Fork it! Fork you.

DR. SCOTT: We came here to discuss Eddie.

COLUMBIA: Eddie! *Shut up bitch or you'll be dessert.*

FRANK: That's a rather tender subject . . . another slice anyone?
*(Sings) And you took the food right out of my mouth, oh it
must have been while you were chewing me.*

COLUMBIA: Excuse me.

(COLUMBIA RUSHES FROM ROOM SCREAMING.)

*What's the matter Columbia? You've eaten Eddie before. But
not with ketchup.*

DR. SCOTT: I knew he was in with a bad crowd. But it was worse than I imagined . . . Aliens!

BRAD & JANET: Dr. Scott! *Janet, Brad, Rocky, Uggh.*

FRANK: Go on, Dr. Scott - or should I say Doctor von Scott?

BRAD: Just what exactly are you implying?

DR. SCOTT: That's alright Brad.

BRAD: But Doctor Scott . . .

DR. SCOTT: That's alright.
(Sings.) From the day he was born
Not the night, but the day.
He was trouble.
Not Monopoly, but trouble.
He was the thorn
Not the rose, but the thorn.
In his mothers side.
Not the back, but the side.
She tried in vain
Not the artery, but the vein.
But he never caused her nothing but shame.
Shame, shame, shame.
He left home the day she died.
It's rockin' Scott.
From the day she was gone
Shoo-bop, shoo-bop, bop or *Suck Dr. Scott's c**k.*
All he wanted
Shoo-bop, shoo-bop, bop or *Suck Dr. Scott's c**k.*
Was rock and roll, porn
Shoo-bop, shoo-bop, bop or *Suck Dr. Scott's c**k.*
And a motorbike.
Vroom-vroom.
Shooting up junk
Shoo-bop, shoo-bop, bop or *Suck Dr. Scott's c**k.*

CRIMINOLOGIST: He was a low-down, cheap, little punk. *Yeah punk.* Taking everyone for a ride.

ALL: When Eddie said
He didn't like his teddy
You knew he was a no-good kid.

But when he threatened your life
With a switch-blade knife

FRANK: What a guy.

JANET: Makes you cry.

DR. SCOTT: Und I did.

(SCENE CHANGES TO COLUMBIA'S BEDROOM.)

COLUMBIA: Everybody shoved him.
I very nearly loved him.
I said, hey listen to me,
Stay sane inside insanity.
But he locked the door
And threw away the key.

(RETURN TO DINING ROOM.)

DR. SCOTT: But he must have been drawn
Shoo-bop, shoo-bop, bop or ***Suck Dr. Scott's c**k.***
Into something
Shoo-bop, shoo-bop, bop or ***Suck Dr. Scott's c**k.***
Making him warn
Shoo-bop, shoo-bop, bop or ***Suck Dr. Scott's c**k.***
me, in a note which reads

ALL: What's it say? What's it say?

EDDIE'S VOICE: I'm out of my head *H-E-D - Head*
Oh hurry, or I may be dead. *Spelled right.*
They mustn't carry out their evil deeds,
Yaaaow.

ALL: When Eddie said he didn't like his teddy
You knew he was a no-good kid.
But when he threatened your life
With a switch-blade knife

FRANK: What a guy.

JANET: Makes you cry.

DR. SCOTT: Und I did.

ALL: When Eddie said he didn't like his teddy
You knew he was a no-good kid.

But when he threatened your life
With a switch-blade knife

FRANK: What a guy.

ALL: Woo woe woe

JANET: Makes you cry.

ALL: Hey hey hey

DR. SCOTT: Und I did.

ALL: *What's for dessert?* EDDIE!

(FRANK PULLS AWAY TABLECLOTH AND REVEALS EDDIE'S
REMAINS IN COFFIN BENEATH TABLE.)

Not meatloaf again?

(JANET SCREAMS AND RUNS INTO ROCKY'S ARMS.)

FRANK: Oh, Rocky, how can you? *Slap that bitch.*

(FRANK SLAPS JANET AND STARTS TO CHASE HER
THROUGH THE CASTLE.)

Which vay? Which vay?

DR. SCOTT: This vay! This vay!

(BRAD FOLLOWS THEM PUSHING DR. SCOTT'S
WHEELCHAIR.)

(MAGENTA IS LAUGHING.)

RIFF-RAFF: Shut-up!

FRANK: (Sings.) I'll tell you once,
Won't tell you twice
You'd better wise up
Janet Weiss.

Your apple pie
Don't taste too nice
You'd better wise up Janet Weiss.

I've laid the seed
It should be all you need.

You're as sensual
As a pencil
Wound up like an "E" or first string.

When we made it
Did ya hear a bell ring?

AUDIENCE RINGS BELL.

FRANK: Y'got a block,
Take my advice.
You'd better wise up,
Janet Weiss.

(THEY HAVE ALL ARRIVED IN THE LAB.)

FRANK: The transducer (He slams the handle.)
Will seduce yah.

(DR. SCOTT, BRAD & JANET FIND THEY ARE STUCK TO THE
FLOOR.)

JANET: My feet – I can't move my feet.

DR. SCOTT: My wheels – my God, I can't move my wheels.

BRAD: It's as if we were glued to the spot. *My socks, I can't move my
socks.*

FRANK: You are – so quake with fear, you tiny fools.

JANET: We're trapped.

FRANK: It's something you'll
get used to.
A mental mind f**k
Can be nice.

JANET: Oh!

DR. SCOTT: You won't find earth people quite the easy mark you imagine. This sonic transducer – it is, I suppose, some kind of audio-vibratory, physiomolecular transport device . . .

BRAD: You mean . . . *A vibrator.*

DR. SCOTT: Yes, Brad, it's something we ourselves have been working on for quite some time. *A perfect vibrator.* But it seems our friend here has found a way of perfecting it. A device which is capable of breaking down solid matter and then projecting it through space, and – who knows – perhaps even time itself!

JANET: You mean he's gonna send us to another planet? *I'll go.*

FRANK: Planet. Schmanet. Janet.

You'd better wise up,
Janet Weiss.
You'd better wise up,
Build your thighs up.
You'd better wise up.

CRIMINOLOGIST: Then she cries out –

JANET: Sto-o-o-o-o-p! *More! More! More!*

FRANK: (Singing.) Don't get hot and flustered –
Use a bit of mustard.

BRAD: You're a hot dog
But you'd better not
Try to hurt her,
Frank Furter.

(FRANK SIGNALS TO MAGENTA. SHE PULLS SWITCH AND BRAD IS TRANSFORMED INTO A STATUE.)

DR. SCOTT: You're a hot dog
But you'd better not
Try to hurt her,
Frank Furter.

(FRANK SIGNALS TO MAGENTA AGAIN. SHE PULLS SWITCH AND DR. SCOTT IS TRANSFORMED INTO A STATUE.)

JANET: You're a hot dog . . .

(FRANK SIGNALS . . . JANET IS A STATUE.)

Who's Tim Curry?

COLUMBIA: My God, I can't stand anymore of this. *Sit down.* First you spurn me for Eddie, then you throw him off like an old overcoat for Rocky. You chew people up then you spit them out again.

AUDIENCE MAKES SPITTING SOUND.

What did you say?

COLUMBIA: I loved you. Do you hear me – I loved you – and what did it get me? Yeah, I'll tell you – a big nothing. You're like a sponge, you take, take, take! You drain others of their love and emotion. Yeah, well, I've had enough. You've got to choose between me and Rocky – so named because of the rocks in his head.

(FRANK SIGNALS TO MAGENTA. SHE PULLS SWITCH. CO-LUMBIA IS TRANSFORMED INTO A STATUE.)

Hefty lefty. Mighty righty.

FRANK: It's not easy having a good time. *Try Disneyland.*

(FRANK SIGNALS AND ROCKY IS A STATUE.)

I've seen better buns at McDonald's.

FRANK: Even smiling makes my face ache. *No wonder, you keep biting your knuckles.* And my children turn on me. Rocky's behaving just the way Eddie did. *Show us your ear, Frank.* Do you think I made a mistake splitting his brain between the two of them?

MAGENTA: I grow veary of this vorld. Vhen shall we return to Transylvania, huh? *Vendesday, ven else?*

FRANK: Magenta, I am indeed grateful to both you and your brother, Riff-Raff. *Woof-Woof* You have both served me well – loyalty such as yours shall not go unrewarded – You will discover when the mood takes me I can be quite generous. *What do you charge for blow-jobs?*

MAGENTA: I ask for nothing, master.

FRANK: And you shall receive it in abundance. *What tastes good on cornflakes?* Come, we are ready for the floorshow.

(FRANK LEAVES LAB IN ELEVATOR.)

(RIFF AND MAGENTA WALK OVER TO STATUE OF DR. SCOTT AND PERFORM "ELBOW HANDSHAKE" AND THEN EXIT LAB.)

(SCENE CHANGES BACK TO CRIMINOLOGIST'S OFFICE.)

CRIMINOLOGIST: And so, by some extraordinary coincidence – fate it seems had decided that Brad and Janet should keep that appointment with their friend, Dr. Everett Scott. But is was to be in a situation which none of them could have possibly foreseen. And just a few hours after announcing their engagement, Brad and Janet had both tasted *Frank's c**k.* forbidden fruit. *Yeah, Frank's c**k.* This in itself was proof that their host was a man of little morals. *Yeah, little morals.* and some persuasion. *Yeah, persuasion.* What further indignities *Sex with _____ [fill in blank].* were they to be subjected to? And what of the floorshow *Yeah, floorshow.* that had been spoken of? *Where do you masturbate?* In an empty house, *When do you masturbate?* in the middle of the night, *The rates are cheaper.* what diabolical plan had seized Frank's crazed imagination? What indeed. From what had gone before, it was clear that this was to be *A picnic.* no picnic! *Oh shit, and I brought the ants.*

(SCENE CHANGES TO THE BALLROOM. FRANK IS PUTTING LAST MINUTE TOUCHES ON THE STATUES HE HAS DRESSED IN CORSETS & GARTERBELTS. MUSIC BEGINS, CURTAINS OPEN. FRANK PULLS SWITCH. COLUMBIA COMES TO LIFE AND SINGS.)

COLUMBIA: It was great when it all began
I was a regular Frankie fan.
But it was over when he had the plan
To start working on a muscle-man
Now the only thing that gives me hope *Is smoking dope.*
Is my love of a certain dope *Yeah, dope.*
Rose tints my world keeps me
Safe from my trouble and pain.

(ROCKY COMES TO LIFE.)

ROCKY: I'm just seven hours old *And can't dance.*
Truly beautiful to behold
And somebody should be told
My libido hasn't been controlled
Now the only thing I've come to trust *Is Janet's bust.*
Is an orgasmic rush of lust *Yeah, rush.*
Rose tints my world keeps me

Safe from my trouble and pain.

(BRAD COMES TO LIFE.)

Can you come on the ceiling?

BRAD: It's beyond me
Help me Mommy
I'll be good you'll see
Take this dream away
What's this, let's see
I feel sexy
What's come over me
Here it comes again.

(JANET COMES TO LIFE.)

JANET: I feel released
Bad times deceased
My confidence has increased
Reality is here
The game has been disbanded
My mind has been expanded
It's a gas that Frankie's landed
His lust is so sincere.

(REAR CURTAINS RISE. FRANK IS STANDING UNDER A
LARGE REPLICA OF RKO RADIO PICTURE TOWER.)

FRANK: Whatever happened to Fay Wray? *She went apeshit.* That deli-
cate satin-draped frame *Close-up.* as it clung to her thigh.
What? The apeshit? How I started to cry *I'd cry too, if I had
apeshit on my thigh.* cause I wanted to be dressed just the same.
So did I, honey. Kick that prick.

(FRANK KICKS LEVER. PROCEEDS DOWN STEPS.)

FRANK: Give yourself over to absolute pleasure
Swim the warm waters of sins of the flesh
Erotic nightmares
Beyond any measure
And sensual daydreams
To treasure forever.
Can't you just see it – Whoa-oh

(FRANK JUMPS INTO THE POOL)

*Waiter, there's a transvestite in my soup. Quiet or everyone
will want one. It's a fruit-filled lifesaver.*

FRANK: Don't dream it, be it.
Don't dream it, be it.
Don't dream it, be it.
Don't dream it, be it.

ALL: Don't dream it, be it.
Don't dream it, be it.
Don't dream it, be it.
Don't dream it, be it.

(BRAD, JANET, ROCKY & COLUMBIA JOIN FRANK IN POOL.)

ALL: Don't dream it, be it.
Don't dream it, be it.
Don't dream it, be it.
Don't dream it, be it.

(DR. SCOTT COMES TO LIFE.)

DR. SCOTT: Ach, we've got to get out of this trap before this decadence saps our wills. I've got to be strong and try to hang on, or else my mind, may well snap *Crackle and pop.* und my life will be lived . . . *OK America, show us your underalls.* for the thrill.

(DR. SCOTT REVEALS FISHNET STOCKING ON HIS LEG.)

BRAD: It's beyond me
Help me mommy

JANET: God bless, Lilly Saint Cyr. *Hey Frank, whose pool is it?*

(FRANK RISES OUT OF POOL ON ROCKY'S SHOULDERS.)

FRANK: My, my, my, my, my, my, my, my, my, my
I'm a wild and an untamed thing.
I'm a bee with a deadly sting.
You get a hit and your mind goes ping
Your heart'll thump and your blood will sing.

So let the party and the sounds rock on.
Gonna shake it till the life has gone.
Rose tint my world
Keep me safe from my trouble and pain.

(FRANK IS NOW ON STAGE AND BECKONS OTHERS TO
JOIN HIM IN DANCE.)

ALL: We're a wild and an untamed thing.
We're a bee with a deadly sting.
You get a hit and your mind goes ping.
You'r heart'll thump and your blood will sing.

So let the party and the sounds rock on
Gonna shake it till the life has gone.
Rose tint my world
Keep me safe from my trouble and pain.

(THEY DANCE ACROSS STAGE. DR. SCOTT IS 'DANCING' IN
HIS WHEELCHAIR.)

ALL: We're a wild and an untamed thing
We're a bee with a deadly sting.
You get a hit and your mind goes ping
Your heart'll thump and your blood will sing.

So let the party and the sounds rock on
Gonna shake it till this life has gone.
Rose tint my world
Keep me safe from my trouble and pain.

(RIFF-RAFF AND MAGENTA ENTER IN SPACE OUTFITS.
RIFF-RAFF IS HOLDING A RAY GUN.)

RIFF-RAFF: (Sings.) Frank N. Furter
It's all over.
Your mission is a failure.
Your life style's too extreme.

I'm your new Commander.
You now are my prisoner.
We return to Transylvania (He turns to Magenta.)
Prepare the transit beam.

FRANK: Wait! I can explain. ***It better be good, you got shot the last time.***

(FRANK WHISPERS TO COLUMBIA AND ROCKY. COLUMBIA
GOES TO FOLLOWSPOT. ROCKY TURNS ON SWITCHES,
MUSIC BEGINS.)

Ladies and gentlemen, for one night and one night only, Alfalfa's shadow.

FRANK: (Sings.) On the day I went away.

ALL: Goodbye

FRANK: Was all I had to say

ALL: Now I

FRANK: Want to come again ***So does Brad.*** and stay

ALL: Oh my, my,

FRANK: Smile and that will mean I may

FRANK: Cause I've seen blue skies
Through the tears in my eyes
And I realize
I'm going home
I'm going home.

Everywhere it's been the same

ALL: Feeling

FRANK: Like I'm outside in the rain

ALL: Wheeling

FRANK: Free to try and find a game

ALL: Dealing

FRANK: Cards for sorrow,
Cards for pain.

AUDIENCE THROWS CARDS.

FRANK: Cause I've seen oh blue skies
Through the tears in my eyes
And I realize
I'm going home.
I'm going home.

MAGENTA: How sentimental. *You bitch.*

RIFF-RAFF: And also presumptuous of you. You see when I said "we" were to return to Transylvania, I referred only to Magenta and myself. I'm sorry however if you found my words misleading. You see you were to remain here in spirit anyway.

DR. SCOTT: Good heavens, that's a laser.

RIFF-RAFF: Yes, Dr. Scott. A laser capable of emitting a beam of pure anti-matter.

BRAD: You mean you're going to kill him? What's his crime? *He served leftover meatloaf.*

DR. SCOTT: You saw what became of Eddie. Society must be protected. *F**k society.*

RIFF-RAFF: Exactly, Dr. Scott. And now Frank N. Furter, your time has come. Say goodbye to all this *Goodbye all of this.* and hello *Hello.* to oblivion. *Hi oblivion, how's the wife and kids?* (pause) *First one to scream gets it right in the tits.*

(COLUMBIA SCREAMS. RIFF-RAFF SHOOTS HER.)

(RIFF-RAFF TURNS BACK TO FRANK. FRANK CLIMBS CUR-
TAIN. RIFF-RAFF SHOOTS HIM. FRANK FALLS TO THE
GROUND DEAD. THE CURTAINS FALL AND COVER FRANK.)

It's curtains for you
Could we have some rope?

(ROPE FALLS ON CURTAIN. ROCKY RUSHES TO THE BODY.
HE PICKS UP FRANK AND CARRIES HIM UP THE TOWER.
RIFF-RAFF KEEPS SHOOTING HIM TILL HE FALLS INTO THE
POOL DEAD.)

BRAD: Good God.

JANET: You've killed them

MAGENTA: But I thought you liked them. They liked you. *Get paranoid Riff.*

RIFF-RAFF: They didn't like me. They never liked me.

DR. SCOTT: You did right.

(RIFF TURNS TOWARD DR. SCOTT.)

Slowly I turn, step by step, inch by inch.

RIFF-RAFF: A decision had to be made.

DR. SCOTT: You're ok by me. *Nanu-Nanu.*

RIFF-RAFF: Dr. Scott, I'm sorry about your nephew.

DR. SCOTT: Eddie? *No, Penelope!* You should leave now Dr. Scott while it's
still possible. We are about to beam the entire house back to the
Planet of Transsexual in the galaxy of Transylvania. *What should
they do?* Go. *When?* Now.

(BRAD, JANET AND DR. SCOTT EXIT.)

*Magenta, do your imitation of a chicken underwater with the
hiccups.*

(MAGENTA LAUGHS.)

RIFF-RAFF: Our noble mission is almost completed my most *Ugly Q-Tip.*
beautiful sister. Soon we will return to the moon-drenched shore
Gitchee-Goomee. of our beloved planet.

MAGENTA: Ah – Sweet Transsexual. *You called.* Land of night. *And high
electric bills.* To sing and dance once more to your dark refrains.
To take that *Starts with an 'S'.* step to the right.

RIFF-RAFF: But it's the pelvic thrust
that really drives you insane.

MAGENTA: And our world will do
the Time Warp again.

(RIFF AND MAGENTA MAKE ONE-HANDED ELBOW SIGN.
DR. SCOTT IS CARRIED FROM CASTLE BY BRAD AND JANET.
THE CASTLE TAKES OFF LIKE A SPACESHIP.)

(SPECIAL NOTE: THIS NEXT SONG HAS BEEN ELIMINATED
FROM THE U.S. VIDEO RELEASE.)

(BRAD & JANET ARE CRAWLING AROUND IN THE FOG.
THEY SING.)

BRAD: I've done a lot
God knows I've tried
To find the truth I've even lied
But all I know is down inside –

I'm bleeding.

JANET: And super heroes
Come to feast
To taste the flesh
Not yet deceased
And all I know
Is still the beast

Is feeding.

(THE SCENE ON THE SCREEN BEGINS TO SPIN – IT TURNS
INTO A GLOBE AND THE CRIMINOLOGIST STOPS ITS SPIN
WITH HIS HAND.)

*He just wiped out _____ . (Fill in least favorite
city.)*

CRIMINOLOGIST: And crawling on the planet's face, some insects called the human
race. Lost in time *What's your favorite TV show?* and lost in
space and meaning. *Close the f**king door.*

(CRIMINOLOGIST EXITS AND CLOSES DOOR.)

THE END

(CAST AND CREDITS ROLL DURING CLOSING REPRISE.)

VOICE OVER: Science Fiction – double-feature
Frank has built and lost his creature.
Darkness has conquered Brad and Janet.
The servant's gone to a distant planet.
Oh – at the late night double-feature
Picture Show – I want to go – Ohh –
To the late night double-feature picture show.

Introduction to the Collector's Guide

In 2014, I was asked to update the Collector's Section of the Rocky Horror Audience Participation Book. I knew it would be a very difficult and rewarding endeavor. I am fortunate to have many friends in the Rocky Horror fan base to help me out. This is by no means a complete index of absolutely every piece of collectable memorabilia available.

Many people tirelessly endeavored to make this guide possible. To all of them I would like to say thank you. Thank you for sharing your knowledge and time to help make this a complete successful project. It is an absolute honor to work with all of you. The original Audience Participation / Collectors Guide introduction included a short statement from Sal Piro, The Rocky Horror Fan Club President. It is only appropriate we echo his sentiments here;

"One of the many joys of being a "Rocky Horror" fans is collecting the products and memorabilia that have been available over the years. Some of these items are readily available in stores or through mail order, others are extremely rare and impossible to find. Not all products have been licensed through the studio-many are bootleg or promotional items. Because of this, it is impossible to list every item ever made. The following guide deals with items related to "The Rocky Horror Picture Show", "Shock Treatment" and "The Rocky Horror Show" (the London, Los Angeles and Broadway productions of the play). Many of the prices listed are estimated based on availability and condition. Obviously, the better condition something is in, the more it is worth. The act that an item is listed with an estimated value does NOT mean that it is available."

The original guide was written well before the internet took off. Back then, there were only a few places to get Rocky Horror collectables. Sal Piro sold items from the fan club, while Bruce Cutter and Mad Man Mike Ellenbogen had mail order companies where you could buy items. You certainly couldn't go out to your nearest shopping mall and get a Rocky Horror T-Shirt. You were lucky if your local record store had a Rocky Horror album or cassette or your local book shop had a Rocky Horror book.

Things have changed. Now, you can find Rocky Horror items at your local clothing store. Rocky Horror has a large online presence, especially on sites like Ebay. Rocky Horror collectables are like any other collectors market. The market goes up and down. The values on some items can fluctuate daily. Therefore, we have decided to leave prices off the audio collectables in this book. It's an ever moving, and ever changing target. Collectables will always be worth what people will pay for them.

My specific area of interest in Rocky Horror collecting was always books and paper. I loved collecting books and magazines associated with Rocky. And because of that love, it's a true honor to be working on a Rocky Horror book. Once again, I simply must take "Don't Dream It... Be It" to heart. I have to stop dreaming of being an author and I have to "Be It". I hope you enjoy this updated version of The Rocky Horror Picture Show Collector's Guide.

Thank you, and remember "Don't Dream It... Be It"

Jim "Cosmo" Hetzer

Author's Note: All items listed were known as of September 1, 2014 and does not include any of the 40th

Important Information:
Within this Collector's Guide we will utilize the following abbreviations:
- DSJ – A Different Set of Jaws
- RHPS -- The Rocky Horror Picture Show
- RHS – The Rocky Horror Show
- HTH -- That's Right He's the Hero
- ST – Shock Treatment
- PS -- Picture Sleeve
- LP – Long Play

ROCKY HORROR BOOKS / SCRIPTS

	Fair / Low	Mint / High
Softcover - The Rocky Horror Picture Show Official Movie Novel	$10.00	$30.00
Hardcover - The Rocky Horror Picture Show Official Movie Novel	$75.00	$100.00
The Rocky Horror Picture Show German Movie Novel	$50.00	$75.00
The Rocky Horror Picture Show Book by Bill Henkin	$5.00	$20.00
The Rocky Horror Picture Show Press Book	$20.00	$35.00
The Rocky Horror Picture Show Press Book 2nd Edition	$20.00	$35.00
The Rocky Horror Picture Show Japanese Press Book	$30.00	$40.00
The Rocky Horror Picture Show Press Kit (1975)	$50.00	$75.00
The Rocky Horror Picture Show Shooting Script	$10.00	$25.00
The Rocky Horror Show Stage Script	$5.00	$15.00
The Rocky Horror Experience	$25.00	$40.00
Shock Treatment Shooting Script	$10.00	$20.00
The Rocky Horror Scrapbook	$75.00	$100.00
The Rocky Horror Scrapbook (Reprint)	$80.00	$125.00
Creatures of the Night by Sal Piro	$15.00	$25.00
Creatures of the Night by Sal Piro (Reprint)	$15.00	$19.95
Creatures of the Night II by Sal Piro	$5.00	$15.00
Creatures of the Night II by Sal Piro (Reprint)	$15.00	$19.95
The Rocky Horror Picture Show Audience Par-tic-i-pation Guide (Original)	$5.00	$15.00
The Rocky Horror Picture Show Audience Par-tic-i-pation Guide (Updated)	$10.00	$14.95
Cosmic Light: The Birth of a Cult Classic - Jim Whittaker	$50.00	$75.00
Rocky Horror: From Concept to Cult - Scott Michaels & David Evans	$10.00	$20.00
The Rocky Horror Show Book - James Harding	$15.00	$30.00
The Rocky Horror Picture Show Original Movie Script 20th Anniversary Edition	$10.00	$20.00
The Rocky Horror Picture Show Official Australian Magazine	$10.00	$25.00
The Rocky Horror Picture Show Italian Book	$15.00	$35.00
Still the Beast is Feeding: Forty Years of Rocky Horror	$10.00	$19.97
Perry Bedden's The Rocky Horror Picture Book	$25.00	$34.95
The Rocky Horror Treasury: A Tribute to the Ultimate Cult Classic Hardcover	$20.00	$27.00
The Brad and Janet Show Shooting Script	$10.00	$20.00
Shock Treatment script pre-Bert Schnick	$15.00	$25.00
Shock Treatment Press Kit	$25.00	$50.00
To Hell and Back (Meatloaf Autobiography)	$10.00	$27.95
Rocky Horror - Mick Rock (Schwarzkopf & Schwarzkopf; hardback)	$150.00	$250.00
Confessions of a Transylvanian - Kevin Theis and Ron Fox (Berwick Court, 2012; paperback)	$10.00	$16.95
Midnight at the Lost and Found - Eric Bradshaw	$5.00	$10.00
Be Just and Fear Not: Memoirs of a Rocky Horror EmCee - Chadwick Cunningham	$7.00	$12.00

	Fair / Low	Mint / High
The Rocky Horror Picture Show Music on Film - Dave Thompson	$5.00	$8.00
Rocky Horror Comic #1	$3.00	$7.00
Rocky Horror Comic #2	$3.00	$7.00
Rocky Horror Comic #3	$5.00	$7.00
Rocky Horror Comic Compilation	$10.00	$15.00
The Book of Sides: Audience Participation "A Formal Format" - Richard David Renda	$10.00	$25.00
RHPS "Non Sognatelo, Siatelo!" - Paolo Belluso & Flavio Merkel (Gammalibri)	$20.00	$35.00
RHPS Edizioni Blues Brothers (Italian mini book, 1991; L10,000, paperback)	$10.00	$20.00
Rocky Horror: 25 anni di cult - Antonella Rotti, Isabella Rotti, and Federico Lamastra	$25.00	$40.00
The Rocky Horror Picture Show and Popular Culture, Edited by Jeffrey Andrew Weinstock	$75.00	$100.00
RHPS Cultographies - Jeffrey Weinstock (Wallflower, 2007, paperback)	$10.00	$20.00
RHPS: 25 Años de Culto - Miguel Angel Parra (Midons Editorial, 2000; paperback)	$15.00	$25.00
Collage of a Life: Memoirs of an artist, actor and humorist - Jonathan Adams	$5.00	$20.00

ROCKY HORROR MAGAZINES

	Fair / Low	Mint / High
The Transylvanian Missing Issues - All 4 of the original Transylvanian, pre-national distribution		
The Transylvanian #1 - Black and white cover. Riff Raff looking out castle	$10.00	$20.00
The Transylvanian #2 - Pink cover with black and white Curry concert photo.	$10.00	$20.00
The Transylvanian #3 - Gold sequin cover with color photo of Curry as Frank N. Furter	$10.00	$30.00
The Transylvanian Special Edition - Announcing the AP Album	$2.00	$5.00
The Transylvanian #4 Announcing the release of 'Shock Treatment'	$2.00	$5.00
Inside Insanity (newsprint)	$2.00	$5.00
Inside Insanity (quality paper)	$5.00	$10.00
The Rocky Horror Collector's Magazine Interviews with O'Brien, Sue Blane, Brian Thompson	$15.00	$30.00
RHPS German Collectors Magazine	$25.00	$40.00
The Rocky Horror Poster Magazine #1	$5.00	$10.00
The Official Rocky Horror Poster Magazine #2	$5.00	$10.00
The Official Rocky Horror Poster Magazine #3	$5.00	$10.00
Rocky Convention 1 Poster/Announcement (A style) — 1979	$10.00	$25.00
Rocky Horror Weekend Poster/Announcement (B style) — 1979	$10.00	$20.00
The Rocky Horror Picture Show Official Australian Magazine	$20.00	$30.00
Dark Refrain- Dark Refrain is a Rocky Horror fanzine	$5.00	$15.00
Dark Refrain II - Dark Refrain is a Rocky Horror fanzine	$5.00	$15.00
Dark Refrain III - Dark Refrain is a Rocky Horror fanzine made up of fiction	$5.00	$15.00

ROCKY HORROR PROGRAMS

	Fair / Low	Mint / High
2nd Official Transylvanian Convention Program	$10.00	$20.00
The Rocky Horror Picture Show 10th Anniversary Program	$20.00	$35.00
The Rocky Horror Picture Show 10th Anniversary Cake Folder	$10.00	$20.00
The Rocky Horror Show L.A. Roxy Cast Press Folder Play logo with the Columbia face logo	$5.00	$10.00
The Rocky Horror Show L.A. Roxy Cast Program	$10.00	$20.00
The Rocky Horror Show Belasco Theater Broadway Cast Playbill	$15.00	$30.00
The Rocky Horror Show Original London Cast Program	$10.00	$15.00
The Rocky Horror Show Souvenir Book and Libretto	$10.00	$25.00
Japanese Souvenir Brochure and Libretto from 1988 Fan Club Tour	$10.00	$35.00

ROCKY HORROR SONGBOOKS

	Fair / Low	Mint / High
The Rocky Horror Show by Richard O'Brien	$15.00	$25.00
The Rocky Horror Show - Piano/Vocal/Organ/Chords	$20.00	$30.00
Richard O'Brien's - The Rocky Horror Show Vocal Selections	$15.00	$20.00
The Rocky Horror Show - The Musicals Collection No.41	$10.00	$20.00
The Rocky Horror Show Song Book	$15.00	$25.00
The Rocky Horror Show Vocal Selections Sing-Along (Wise Publications)	$15.00	$25.00

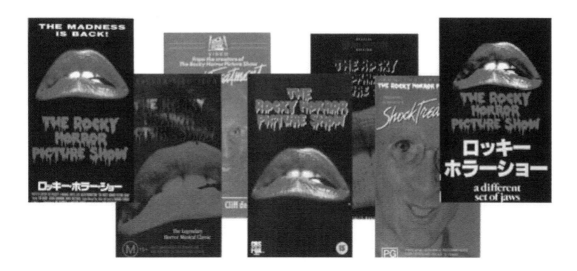

ROCKY HORROR VIDEO

	Fair / Low	Mint / High
The Rocky Horror Picture Show U.S. Release	$1.00	$10.00
The Rocky Horror Picture Show British Release (Contains the original ending.)	$5.00	$20.00
The Rocky Horror Picture Show Japanese Release	$15.00	$30.00
Shock Treatment	$5.00	$15.00
The Rocky Horror Picture Show DVD	$3.00	$5.00
Shock Treatment DVD	$5.00	$7.00
25th Anniversary The Rocky Horror Picture Show and Shock Treatment 2 pack DVD	$15.00	$20.00
The Rocky Horror Picture Show Blu-Ray (featuring the NDA Cast)	$15.00	$25.00

ROCKY HORROR BUTTONS

	Fair / Low	Mint / High
The Button Up Company (An assortment of 23 different full color buttons)	$1.00	$5.00
A & B Creations (Set of 6 full color large buttons)	$10.00	$20.00
Special Square Buttons	$5.00	$10.00
The Rocky Horror Picture Show 10th Anniversary Button	$5.00	$10.00
Shock Treatment Button	$5.00	$10.00
Budweiser/RHPS Button (1996 Budweiser/RHPS Halloween Promotion) (3" round)	$1.00	$5.00

ROCKY HORROR LOBBY CARDS

	Fair / Low	Mint / High
U.S. 10x11 Inch Set of Ten Different Cards	$25.00	$60.00
U.S. 8x10 Inch Set of Ten Different Cards	$20.00	$40.00
British Lobby Cards 11 x 14	$25.00	$50.00
British Lobby Cards 8 x 10	$20.00	$40.00
The Rocky Horror Picture Show - Mexican Lobby Cards	$195.00	$220.00
Rocky Horror Picture Show - Cinema Window Card	$25.00	$40.00

ROCKY HORROR FILM

	Fair / Low	Mint / High
Super 8 Sound Digest Version of The Rocky Horror Picture Show	$30.00	$60.00
The Rocky Horror Picture Show Preview Trailer		
• Super 8	$25.00	$45.00
• 16mm	$50.00	$75.00
• 35mm.	$75.00	$125.00

	Fair / Low	Mint / High
The Rocky Horror Picture Show		
• Full film on 16mm film	$350.00	$1,000.00
• Full film on 35mm film	$500.00	$2,000.00
• 35mm Frame from The Rocky Horror Picture Show	$5.00	$10.00
Shock Treatment Preview Trailer		
• Super 8	$20.00	$25.00
• 16mm	$25.00	$45.00
• 35mm	$35.00	$75.00
Shock Treatment		
• 16mm	$200.00	$400.00
• 35mm	$800.00	$1,000.00

ROCKY HORROR POSTCARDS
AND GREETING CARDS

	Fair / Low	Mint / High
LIPS and Film Logo	$1.00	$2.00
Chair Scene (Color)	$1.00	$2.00
Throne Scene Postcard	$1.00	$2.00
Dr. Frank-N-Furter	$1.00	$2.00
Peter Hinwood as Rocky Horror (a creation) Postcard	$1.50	$3.00
British Film Poster (soundtrack design) Postcard (5-7/8" x 4-1/8")	$1.50	$3.00
British Film Poster (soundtrack design) Postcard (5-3/8" x 3-3/4")	$1.50	$3.00
He's the Hero Poster Postcard	$1.50	$3.00
He's the Hero Poster Postcard (German / Glossy finish)	$1.50	$3.00
Lips/Logo Film Poster Postcard (Humour la Carte – France)	$1.50	$3.00
Lips/Logo Film Poster Postcard (Ludlow Sales, New York)	$1.50	$3.00
Lips/Logo Film Poster Postcard (Metro Music, Printed in the E.E.C.)	$1.50	$3.00
Lips/Logo Postcard (Santoro Graphics Ltd., England)	$1.50	$3.00
Throne Scene (Black and White) Postcard (Editions cinema -- France) Printed vertically	$1.50	$3.00
RHPS/Frank N. Furter (Roxy Pose) Postcard (Underground)	$1.50	$3.00
Frank N. Furter (color face shot) Postcard (Printed in the E.E.C.)	$1.50	$3.00
Frank N. Furter, Columbia and Magenta (Creation Scene) Postcard (Underground)	$1.50	$3.00
Frank N. Furter, Columbia and Magenta (Creation Scene) Postcard (Palm Pictures b&w)	$1.50	$3.00
Rocky Horror 10th Anniversary Postcard (Cake Poster - Imprime in C.E.E.)	$1.50	$3.00
Crabwalk Greeting Cards (Set of 10 assorted cards with envelopes in plastic box)	$30.00	$60.00
Rocky Horror Christmas Cards	$10.00	$14.50

	Fair / Low	Mint / High
RHPS Postcards: PC2069 - Frank "Come on then"	$1.50	$2.50
RHPS Postcards: PC2113 - Frank "I'm just a sweet Transvestite"	$1.50	$2.50
RHPS Postcards: PC2084 - Throne Scene (says TRHPS across bottom of card)	$1.50	$2.50
RHPS Postcards: PC8300 - Frank in front of throne (Riff, Magenta and Columbia)	$1.50	$2.50
RHPS Postcards: PC8301 - Floorshow Kickline	$1.50	$2.50
RHPS Postcards: PC2129 - Frank after floorshow (just after Riff and Magenta appear)	$1.50	$2.50
RHPS Postcards: PC102 - Rocky Horror Picture Show Album Cover Artwork	$1.50	$2.50
RHPS Postcards: PC7701 - RHPS/Lips and Logo	$1.50	$2.50
RHPS Postcards: PC7702 - Time Warp Dance Chart	$1.50	$2.50
RHPS Postcards: PC7703 - Columbia (in floorshow costume)	$1.50	$2.50
RHPS Greeting Cards: GC7601 - RHPS/Lips and Logo	$2.00	$4.00
RHPS Greeting Cards: GC7602 - Frank with rubber gloves	$2.00	$4.00
RHPS Greeting Cards: GC7603 - RHPS/Columbia/Rocky's creation	$2.00	$4.00
RHPS Greeting Cards: GC7604 - Riff and coffin - beginning of Time Warp	$2.00	$4.00

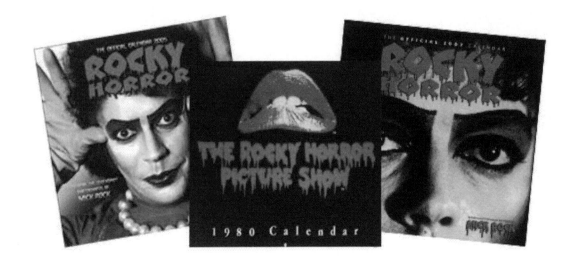

ROCKY HORROR CALENDARS

	Fair / Low	Mint / High
Rocky Horror Picture Show 1980 Calendar - 12 full color photos.	$15.00	$30.00
RHPS 1990 Calendar (Portal)	$5.00	$20.00
RHPS 1992 Calendar: The Year of the Floorshow (Landmark)	$5.00	$20.00
RHPS In Celebration of the 20th Anniversary 1996 Calendar with pull-out poster	$5.00	$20.00
RHPS 25 Years of Absolute Pleasure! 2001 Calendar (Entertainment Calendars)	$5.00	$15.00
Rocky Horror: The Official 2003 Calendar (Mick Rock; Slow Dazzle)	$5.00	$20.00
Rocky Horror: The Official 2004 Calendar (Mick Rock; Slow Dazzle)	$5.00	$20.00
Rocky Horror: The Official 2005 Calendar (Mick Rock; Slow Dazzle)	$5.00	$20.00
Rocky Horror: The Official 2006 Calendar (Mick Rock; Slow Dazzle)	$5.00	$20.00
Rocky Horror: The Official 2007 Calendar (Mick Rock; Slow Dazzle)	$5.00	$20.00
Rocky Horror: The Official 2008 Calendar (Mick Rock; Slow Dazzle)	$5.00	$20.00
RHPS: A 16-Month 2008 Calendar (Day Dream)	$5.00	$15.00
Rocky Horror: The Official 2009 Calendar (Mick Rock; Slow Dazzle)	$5.00	$20.00

ROCKY HORROR - MISC.

	Fair / Low	Mint / High
Rocky Horror Guitar -- 2009 - (Hetzer Guitar Company)		$500.00
Headliners XL (Full Set of 6)		$100.00
Frank Headliner - Individual		$30.00
Riff-Raff Headliner - Individual		$30.00
Magenta Headliner - Individual		$30.00
Rocky Headliner - Individual		$30.00
Janet Headliner - Individual		$30.00
Columbia Headliner - Individual		$30.00
Headliners (Full Set – Prototypes – Only One Known Copy Exists)		$250.00
Columbia - Vital Toys	$10.00	$30.00
Vital Toys 3 figure set (Frank, Riff, Columbia)	$30.00	$50.00
Vital Toys 3 bendable figure set (Frank, Riff, Columbia)	$30.00	$50.00
Spencer's Frank N Furter Doll (Sings Time Warp)	$60.00	$100.00
Spencer's RHPS Light Up Shadow Box with Lips	$20.00	$50.00
Frank-n-Furter Rubber Duck (Multiple Versions Exist)	$5.00	$12.00
Frank-n-Furter - Vital Toys	$15.00	$30.00
Riff-Raff - Vital Toys	$15.00	$30.00
RHPS Trivia Game	$40.00	$75.00
RHPS Icons Sticker	$2.00	$4.00
Come on Then (Frank N. Furter/Tim Curry) Sticker		$3.00
Frank Face Rub On - White		$4.00
Frank Face Rub On - Red		$4.00
Brad Face Rub On - Black		$4.00
Brad Face Rub On - White		$4.00
Rocky & Janet Rub On - Black		$4.00
Rocky & Janet Rub On - White		$4.00
Riff Raff Face Rub On - Black		$4.00
Riff Raff Face Rub On - White		$4.00
RHPS 20th Anniversary Bumper Sticker		$4.00
RHPS/Celluloid Jam Bumper Sticker		$1.00
RHPS/Lips Embroidered Magnet -- (3" x 1.5")	$1.50	$5.00
RHPS 25 Years of Absolute Pleasure – (2" x 3")	$1.50	$5.00
RHPS Lips/Logo Magnet -- (2" x 3")	$1.50	$5.00
Frank N. Furter (Tim Curry) Face Magnet – (2" x 3")	$1.50	$5.00
RHPS Lips/Logo (circle design) Magnet -- (2.5" x 2.5")	$1.50	$5.00
Riff Raff (Richard O'Brien) Face Magnet – (2" x 3")	$1.50	$5.00
RHPS 25th Anniversary Hard Rock Casino $5 Chip	$10.00	$15.00
RHPS 25th Anniversary Hard Rock Casino $25 Chip	$120.00	$200.00

	Fair / Low	Mint / High
Hard Rocky Casino - Blackjack Table Cloth	$100.00	$137.00
RHS Rolling Papers	$5.00	$10.00
Rocky Interactive Horror Show CD-ROM (1999)	$10.00	$20.00
Crazed Imagination Fanzine (106 Issues)	$5.00	$10.00
RHPS Lips T-Shirt Iron On	$10.00	$25.00
RHPS Frank Don't Dream It T-Shirt Iron On	$10.00	$20.00
RHS - Souvenir Mirror sold on the Hanley UK Tour. (Roxy Head & Timewarp)	$20.00	$50.00
RHPS - 1990 Chocolate Lips. Promo for the video release (Very Rare)	$5.00	$20.00
Full Set of 60 Color Trading Cards	$25.00	$35.00
Trading Card Display Box	$40.00	$60.00
Trading Card Unopened Wax Box of Trading Cards (LIPS)	$20.00	$35.00
The Rocky Horror Show Columbia Logo Face Mask	$15.00	$30.00
Shock Treatment Cosmo Face Mask	$15.00	$40.00

ROCKY HORROR POSTERS

	Fair / Low	Mint / High
RHPS - Original One-Sheet - Style A	$15.00	$75.00
RHPS - British Quad (Horizontal One Sheet)	$35.00	$100.00
RHPS - Style B	$25.00	$75.00
RHPS - Japanese Release Poster.	$50.00	$100.00
RHPS - Japanese Release Poster.1998 Fan Club Tour	$50.00	$100.00
RHPS - 1975 US - Style B 30x40	$40.00	$60.00
RHPS - 1975 - Australian Daybill (long and skinny) White poster with throne scene at top	$20.00	$40.00
RHPS – 1977 - Insert poster white with red text. (Odd lips) Both HTH & DSJ On cardstock	$35.00	$50.00
RHPS – 1978 Soundtrack Promo Poster white background. Red and black text)	$25.00	$40.00
RHPS - 10th Anniversary Cake Poster / No Ad	$35.00	$200.00
RHPS - 10th Anniversary Cake Poster / ad for the NY con	$20.00	$150.00
RHPS - 1984 Australian Video Release promo red border with (DSJ)	$25.00	$35.00
RHPS - Soundtrack Album Promo Available At Last	$25.00	$45.00
RHPS - Commercial Frank Roxy pose poster UK	$15.00	$25.00
RHPS - Chair Scene (White background with full color chair scene and red logo)	$20.00	$35.00
RHPS - Fay Wray - Tim Curry in the Fay Wray pose.	$15.00	$25.00
RHPS - Collage Poster (Several full color photos from the film.)	$15.00	$25.00
RHPS - Collage Poster (Same poster as at bottom of preceding page without the film logo on it.)	$25.00	$40.00
RHPS - Come Up to The Lab	$15.00	$25.00
RHPS - The Transylvanian Convention Poster Black and white Mick Rock photo	$25.00	$35.00
RHPS - Soundtrack Poster Advertising RHPS and ST	$10.00	$35.00
RHPS - Greeting Card Poster	$20.00	$30.00
RHPS - Curry Casting Chair	$25.00	$40.00

	Fair / Low	Mint / High
RHPS – Lips on white background with purple and red text)	$25.00	$35.00
RHPS - Spanish white poster with the Lips/on top of the legs photo and purple text	$30.00	$40.00
RHPS - 1990 - 15th Anniversary Cake poster	$20.00	$30.00
RHPS - 2000 - Lips (DSJ) Funky Enterprises	$5.00	$20.00
RHPS - Style B - Half Sheet (Horizontal instead of vertical) on thick cardboard stock	$35.00	$50.00
RHPS - 1989 – (DSJ) reproduction by Portal Publications M2-501	$10.00	$20.00
RHPS - 1996 – Promo shot of Frank in the Ballroom (w/tongue sticking out)	$5.00	$15.00
RHPS - 1990 US Video Release Promo Poster (Dream It in Your Living Room...)	$5.00	$20.00
RHPS - Lips Australian Daybill	$20.00	$30.00
RHPS - Australian One Sheet Red Background - Lips Different Set Of Jaws	$30.00	$50.00
RHPS - Mexican One Sheet – (DSJ) in Spanish	$40.00	$80.00
RHPS - Argentina One Sheet - (DSJ) in Spanish	$40.00	$80.00
RHPS - Danish One Sheet – Lips - (DSJ) in Danish	$30.00	$60.00
RHPS - Lips Different Set of Jaws Promo poster for Films Inc.	$30.00	$40.00
RHPS - Style B Insert Poster (the same as a Daybill poster) USA on heavy cardboard stock	$35.00	$50.00
RHPS - 1995 20th Anniversary poster (Frank and gang)	$10.00	$20.00
RHPS - 1990 15th Anniversary -- Frank with hand over head Egyptian style	$10.00	$20.00
RHPS - Audience Participation Poster	$25.00	$40.00
ST - One-sheet	$20.00	$35.00
ST - Red poster with photo of Richard O'Brien as Cosmo McKinley	$20.00	$35.00
ST - Australian Daybill poster (long skinny type poster)	$20.00	$40.00
ST - Australian One Sheet (Cosmo head. text in black and yellow)	$25.00	$40.00
ST - Half Sheet US on thick cardboard stock	$25.00	$40.00
ST - 1981 insert Poster USA on heavy cardboard stock	$25.00	$35.00
ST - Italian Promo Poster features "The Rocky Horror Picture Show	$20.00	$50.00
RHS - 1975 Original Japanese Production promo poster (features the Roxy Columbia Artwork)	$35.00	$75.00
RHS - 1991 Subway poster (Anthony Head / Sweet Transvestite single and the show UK)	$30.00	$50.00
RHS - Roxy Cast Album Promo Poster	$25.00	$40.00
RHS - King's Road Theatre Poster from London	$50.00	$75.00

ROCKY HORROR AUDIO

ROCKY HORROR SHOW – ORIGINAL LONDON CAST
* UK 1973 UK Records, UKAL 1006 Demo Test Pressing LP
  Notes: "The Rocky Horror Show Original London Cast" Handwritten on a purple inner label sticker.
  Also states "Factory Sample Not for Sale"

- UK 1973 UK Records, UKAL 1006 promotional LP
  Notes: sticker on cover states "Promotional Copy Not for Sale"

- UK 1973 UK Records, UKAL 1006 promotional LP
  Notes: "US promotion7 campaign" released to coincide with the New York opening of The RHS at The Belasco Theatre - includes a US press release sheet and promotional LP folder. Also contains a glossy 8' x10' publicity photo of Tim Curry as Frank from London!

- UK 1973 UK Records, UKAL 1006 white label LP
  Notes: first general UK pressing containing the original sound mix with minor engineering flaws. Label is plain white and is unlike all other commercial UK Records pressings

- UK 1973 UK Records, UKAL 1006 LP
  Notes: first general UK pressing containing the original sound mix with minor engineering flaws. Album jacket is printed on a flimsy quality cardboard stock Dennis Cowan from "The Bonzos" plays on bass.

- UK 1973 UK Records, UKAL 1006 LP
  Notes: another UK pressing containing the original sound mix with minor engineering flaws. Album jacket is printed on a thicker heavy cardboard stock. Back contains minor differences in the text lay out to above pressing

- AUSTRALIA 1973 DECCA / EMI Records, SKLA.7705 LP
  Notes: early Australian pressing containing the original sound mix, label is dark purple. "Decca" logo replaces "UK" Records logo on bottom right corner of album cover

- NEW ZEALAND 1973 Phonogram Records, 2330-103 LP
  Notes: New Zealand pressing containing the original sound mix, "Phonogram Distribution" details printed on back

- SOUTH AFRICA 1974 Interpak / UK Records, 2329-001 LP
  Notes: South African pressing containing the original sound mix, label is silver featuring black text and "UK Records" logo

- UK 1974 UK Records, UKAL 1015 LP
  Notes: this second release of the album was remixed to improve some minor original engineering flaws. All future releases contain this newly mastered mix

- UK 1974 UK / Polydor Records, UKAL-SUPER-1015 LP
  Notes: second pressing of the newly remixed version, label is blue and lay-out of text has been rearranged

- JAPAN 1975 King Records, KI 7512 (SLC544) white label promo LP
  Notes: first Japanese release to coincide with the 1975 stage tour. Includes Japanese 'Obi' Strip and a fold-out photo lyric insert booklet

- JAPAN 1975 King Records, KI 7512 (SLC544) LP
  Notes: first Japanese release to coincide with the 1975 stage tour. Includes Japanese 'Obi' Strip and a fold-out photo lyric insert booklet

- JAPAN 1976 UK Records/Polydor K.K. Japan, MW 2142 LP
  Notes: re-release to coincide with the 1976 Japanese stage tour. Includes Japanese 'Obi' Strip and a fold-out photo lyric insert booklet (featuring lyrics translated completely into Japanese) Back of album jacket is also unique featuring 2 seldom seen Orig London cast photos!

- UK 1989 First Night Records, SCENE 17 LP
  Notes: 1989 re-release with original cover art. "1st Night Records" logo replaces "UK" Records on the bottom right hand corner of the album cover.

- GERMANY 1989 First Night Records, 374921 LP
  Notes: 1989 re-release with original cover art

THE THEATER UPSTAIRS PRODUCTION OF THE RHS FEATURING THE ORIGINAL LONDON CAST

- UK 1987 Dojo Records, DOJOLP 54 white label test pressing LP
  Notes: 1987 re-release featuring new black cover artwork, features 'proof' uncut and unglued sleeve.

- UK 1987 Dojo Records, DOJOLP 54 LP
  Notes: 1987 re-release featuring new black cover artwork. Stars names also added to cover with the caption "IT WAS GREAT WHEN IT ALL BEGAN" Vinyl groove etchings: Side A: "A PORKY PRIME CUT" Side 2: just the words "PORKY" & "ORLAKE" [NB: "Porky" is actually the legendary hallmark of George Peckham, a record cutter from the UK who seems to have cut masters for almost every band in Britain over the last 30 years.

- GERMANY 1987 Teldec Records, 6.26907 LP
  Notes: 1987 re-release featuring new black cover artwork as above but pressed in Germany.

FROM THE ORIGINAL LONDON CAST RECORDING OF THE ROCKY HORROR SHOW UKAL 1006

- UK 1973 UK Records, ZXDR 54070 / XZEFF 3011
  Demonstration white label 7", generic "UK Records" sleeve,
  Time Warp (3:30) / Sweet Transvestite * Touch-A-Touch-A-Touch-A-Touch Me 33 1/3 rpm
  Notes: 3 track promotional sampler from the Original London cast LP. Side 1 or 2 are not specified and it does not contain official UK Records catalogue numbers. Label states:" Produced 1973 King of England B. V. Druid Crest Music. Arranger: Richard Hartley"

THE ORIGINAL LONDON CAST OF THE ROCKY HORROR SHOW FEATURING TIM CURRY

- UK 1974 UK Records, UK67 demonstration 7", generic "UK Records" sleeve,
  Sweet Transvestite (3:20) / Time Warp 45rpm
  Notes: label states "Demonstration Sample Not for Sale to the General Public". Printed release date is 10-5-74. Produced by Jonathan King.

- UK 1974 UK Records, UK67 7", generic "UK Records" sleeve
  Sweet Transvestite (3:20) / Time Warp 45rpm Notes: *Produced by Jonathan King.*

TOUCH-A TOUCH-A TOUCH-A TOUCH ME FROM THE ROCKY HORROR SHOW - BINZI

- UK 1975 Antic Records, K 11522 7", generic "Antic Records" sleeve,
  Touch-A Touch-A Touch-A Touch Me (3:08) /
  Touch-A Touch-A Touch-A Touch Me (Instrumental) (3:08) 45rpm, stereo
  Notes: all new version (not from the Original London Cast recording) sung by Belinda Sinclair (aka Binzi) after succeeding the role of Janet from Julie Covington. Produced by Andrew O'Bonzo for Rich Teaboy Productions. Music arranged by John Sinclair.

ACARICIAME, ACARICIAME, ACARICIAME - BINZI

- ARGENTINA 1975 Atlantic Records, 32.348 7", generic "Music-Hall" sleeve
  Touch-A Touch-A Touch-A Touch Me (3:05) /
  Touch-A Touch-A Touch-A Touch Me (Instrumental) (3:05) 45rpm, stereo
  Notes: all new version (not from the Original London Cast recording) sung by Belinda Sinclair (aka Binzi) after succeeding the role of Janet from Julie Covington. Produced by Andrew O'Bonzo for Rich Teaboy Productions. Music arranged by John Sinclair. Text on label is entirely in Spanish. Label states:"Cantado En Ingles"(Sung In English). Distributed through Music-Hall.

TOUCH-A TOUCH-A TOUCH-A TOUCH ME FROM THE ROCKY HORROR SHOW - BINZI

- TURKEY 1975 Melodi Records, 75507 7" PS
  Touch-A Touch-A Touch-A Touch Me (3:08) / Touch-A Touch-A Touch-A Touch Me (Instrumental) (3:08) 45rpm, stereo
  Notes: new recording (not from the Original London Cast recording) sung by Belinda Sinclair (aka Binzi) Scarce Turkish pressing in exclusive cartoon picture sleeve drawn by "Melih". Produced by Andrew O'Bonzo for Rich Teaboy Productions. Music arranged by John Sinclair.

SWEET TRANSVESTITE FROM THE ROCKY HORROR SHOW – ZIGGY BYFIELD

- JAPAN 1975 Seven Seas Records, TOP-1964 promotional 7" PS
  Sweet Transvestite (3:34) / I'm Going Home (3:29) 45rpm, stereo
  Notes: includes 2 bonus b/w publicity photos from original Japanese production. Japanese promo ink stamp on label. Recorded by "A Style Records" Great Britain, Manufactured by King Records, Japan. Song lyrics printed in English on back sleeve, jukebox cut-out hole.

- JAPAN 1975 Seven Seas Records, TOP-1964 7" PS
Sweet Transvestite (3:34) / I'm Going Home (3:29) 45rpm, stereo
Notes: all new recording by Ziggy Byfield who succeeded the role of Frank in London in 1975. Released during the 1975 Japanese tour of The RHS where he reprised the role. Recorded by "A Style Records" Great Britain, Manufactured by King Records, Japan. Song lyrics printed in English on back sleeve, jukebox cut-out hole.

THE ROCKY HORROR SHOW ORIGINAL LONDON CAST EP
- JAPAN 1976 UK Records / Polydor K.K, Japan, KI 2209 promotional white label 7" PS
Science Fiction-Double Feature (3:30) / Sweet Transvestite (3:22)
Touch-A Touch-A Touch-A Touch Me (2:31) / I'm Going Home (2:10) 33 1/3 rpm, stereo,
*Notes: 4 track promo sampler taken from the Original London
Cast album. Inner label states: "DJ Copy Not For Sale" Japan only release*

TOUCH-A TOUCH-A TOUCH-A TOUCH ME FROM THE ROCKY HORROR SHOW – BELINDA SINCLAIR
- JAPAN 1976 HMV/Victor Records, JET-2331 7" PS
Touch-A Touch-A Touch-A Touch Me (3:08) / Touch-A Touch-A Touch-A Touch Me Instrumental (3:09) 45rpm, stereo,
*Notes: produced by John Sinclair for Rich Teaboy Productions.
Song lyrics printed in Japanese and English on back of cover insert. This was the Japanese re-issue of the original 1975 Binzi "Antic Records" release, jukebox cut-out hole*

- AUSTRALIA 1976 Victor Records/Leeds Music Pty Ltd,
JET-2331 promotional white label 7" PS
Touch-A Touch-A Touch-A Touch Me (3:08) / Touch-A Touch-A Touch-A Touch Me Instrumental (3:09) 45rpm, stereo
Notes: produced by John Sinclair for Rich Teaboy Productions. This was presumably an Australian promo copy as the 7" was never actually released by the record company, jukebox cut-out hole

TOUCH-A, TOUCH-A, TOUCH-A, TOUCH ME – JANET FROM THE ROCKY HORROR SHOW THE RICHARD O'BRIEN CRUSADE
- UK 1979 Rich Teaboy Records, TEA 001 7" PS
Touch Me (2:57) / Over At The Frankenstein Place (2:32) 45rpm, stereo
Notes: all new version of the original 1975 Binzi recording. Often referred to as the "Disco Version" Produced with "The Andrew O'Bonzo Pillar Of Sound" on their own independent "The Rich Tea Boy Label"

THE ROCKY HORROR SHOW – ORIGINAL ROXY CAST
- USA 1974 A&M/ ODE Records Inc, SP 77026 promotional LP, gatefold cover
Notes: promo sticker on cover. Features cast pics on gatefold cover, plus Frank cardboard cut-out. Also includes 24 page photo/ lyric booklet! "Promotion Copy" printed on inner label

- USA 1974 A&M/ ODE Records Inc, 77026 LP, gatefold cover
Notes: features cast pics on gatefold cover, plus Frank cardboard cut-out. Label contains plain ODE label art.

- USA 1974 A&M/ ODE Records Inc, 77026 LP, gatefold cover
Notes: features cast pics on gatefold cover, plus Frank cardboard cut-out. Label contains Trixie image art

- USA 1974 ODE Records, ODE-9009 LP, gatefold cover
Notes: features cast pics on gatefold cover, plus Frank cardboard cut-out.

- USA 1974 ODE/ Jem Records, ODE-9009 LP, gatefold cover
*Notes: second pressing which does not include Frank cut-out.
Inner sleeve bears Frank photo & lyrics.*

- UK 1974 ODE Records, ODE 77026 LP, gatefold cover
Notes: does not include Frank cut-out. Inner sleeve bears Frank photo & lyrics

- CANADA 1974 ODE / Epic Records, ODE 77026 LP, gatefold cover
Notes: cast pics on gatefold cover, includes Frank cardboard cut-out

- AUSTRALIA 1974 A&M/ODE, ODL 35304 white label test pressing LP
  Notes: no cover sleeve or label artwork. Label only states title and catalogue number and name of record label. Distributed by Festival Records

- AUSTRALIA 1974 A&M / Festival Records, L 35304 LP, gatefold cover
  Notes: cast pics on gatefold cover, includes Frank cardboard cut-out

- NEW ZEALAND 1974 A&M / Festival Records, L 35304 LP, gatefold cover
  Notes: cast pics on gatefold cover, includes Frank cardboard cut-out

- JAPAN 1975 King Records, SP 77026 LP, gatefold cover
  Notes: cast pics on gatefold cover, plus Frank cardboard cut-out

- SPAIN 1975 Ariola Ed Espanola, SP 77026 LP, gatefold cover
  Notes: cast pics on gatefold cover.

- UK 1987 ODE/ Pacific Records, ODE 9009 LP, gatefold cover
  Notes: inner sleeve bears Frank photo & lyrics -no Frank cut-out LP Inserted into The Rocky Horror "Say It!" LP Box Set (UK 1988 Pacific Records, RHBX1)

- USA 1974 A&M/ ODE Records Inc, SP 77026 promotional LP, gatefold cover
  Notes: promo sticker on cover. Features cast pics on gatefold cover, plus Frank cardboard cut-out. Also includes 24 page photo/ lyric booklet! "Promotion Copy" printed on inner label. Comes in a black and white "ODE" inner sleeve

- UK 1988 ODE/ Pacific Records, ODE 9009 LP, gatefold cover
  Notes: inner sleeve bears Frank photo & lyrics -no Frank cut-out. LP Inserted into The Rocky Horror Show Album Box Set (UK 1988 Pacific Records, RHBXLP1) The 1987 & 1988 UK re-issues are actually both different pressings specifically released for the 2 different UK LP box sets. Both pressings show a different "Pacific" logo on the back of the sleeve

- USA 1989 Rhino Records, R1-70090 LP
  Notes: new pressing on Rhino. Spine misspells Tim Curry as "Time Curry", does not include Frank cut-out. Inner sleeve bears Frank photo & lyrics.

TIM CURRY AND THE ORIGINAL ROXY CAST
- USA 1974 A&M/ ODE Records Inc, ODE-66103 promotional 7"
  Sweet Transvestite (stereo) (3:20) / Sweet Transvestite (mono) (3:20) 45rpm, stereo/mono
  Notes: Released in both a generic ""Ode"" sleeve and a picture sleeve. The picture sleeve erroneously states "I'm Going Home" is on the B side. Cut-out jukebox hole

- USA 1974 A&M/ ODE Records Inc, ODE-66103-S 7" PS
  Sweet Transvestite (3:20) / I'm Going Home (3:10) 45rpm, stereo

- UK 1974 A&M/ ODE Records Inc, ODS-66103 demonstration
  7", generic "A&M sleeve", Sweet Transvestite (3:20) / I'm Going Home (3:10) 45rpm, stereo
  Notes: "Promotion Copy Not For Sale" printed on label with large red "A" printed across centre

- GERMANY 1974 A&M/ ODE Records, 13-693-AT 7" PS
  Sweet Transvestite (3:20) / I'm Going Home (3:10) 45rpm, stereo

- AUSTRALIA 1974 A&M/ ODE Records, K-5742 7", generic "A&M sleeve"
  Sweet Transvestite (3:20) / I'm Going Home (3:10) 45rpm, stereo

- NEW ZEALAND 1974 A&M/ ODE Records, ODK 5742 7", generic "A&M sleeve"
  Sweet Transvestite (3:20) / I'm Going Home (3:10) 45rpm, stereo

ORIGINAL ROXY CAST / ORIGINAL FILM SOUNDTRACK

* USA 1986 ODE Records Inc, PRCC-11 promotional 7", generic sleeve,
  The Time Warp (Roxy Cast) (3:57) / The Time Warp (Film Soundtrack) (3:15) 45rpm, stereo,
  Notes: cut-out jukebox hole, catalogue # etched into vinyl

ROCKY HORROR SHOW (ORIGINAL AUSTRALIAN CAST ALBUM)

* AUSTRALIA 1974 Festival Records, L 35231 promotional LP Gatefold cover
  Notes gatefold features cast photos & lyrics. Inner record label is blue and contains a red "Sample Record Not For Sale" sticker.

* AUSTRALIA 1974 Festival Records, L 35231 LP, gatefold cover
  Notes gatefold features cast photos & lyrics. Inner record label is blue.

* NEW ZEALAND 1974 Festival Records, L 35231 LP, gatefold cover
  Notes gatefold features cast photos & lyrics. Text is laid out differently on inner blue record label

* USA 1975 Elephant Records / General Recording Corp, ELA 7000 LP
  Notes: budget price US re-issue without gatefold cover. "Suggested Retail $3.29" printed on front cover. Vinyl groove etchings: Side A &B: "Sound Pit"

* THE ROCKY HORROR BAND
  Netherlands 1976 Phillips Records 6012 609 7"Single PS
  Die Tijd Step (Time Warp) 3:13/Hot Patootie (Hot Patootie, Bless My Soul) 2:25
  Notes: recording by the cast of the 1976 Dutch production

* USA 1975 Elephant Records / General Recording Corp, ELA 7000 LP
  Notes: second pressing of the low priced US re-issue without gatefold cover. Text lay out on the record label is noticeably different and the LP is actually pressed on much thicker, better quality vinyl "Suggested Retail $3.29" printed on front cover. Vinyl groove etchings: Side A &B: "Sound Pit".

* AUSTRALIA 1989 Festival Records, L 35231 LP, gatefold cover
  Notes gatefold features cast photos & lyrics. Inserted into The Rocky Horror [Australian] Box Set (1989 Festival Records, L80891/4).

* AUSTRALIA 1974 Festival Records, K-5641 7", generic "Festival Records" sleeve
  Time Warp (3:12) / Whatever Happened To Saturday Night (2:06) 45rpm, stereo
  Notes: both tracks taken from The Rocky Horror Show Original Australian Cast LP This is the only cast album to re-title "Hot Patootie" as such.

THE ROCKY HORROR SHOW (ORIGINAL BRAZILIAN CAST ALBUM)

* *BRAZIL 1975 Som Livre Records, 410.6005 LP, gatefold cover*
  Notes: gatefold includes cast photos. Also contains original insert tour program which includes complete lyrics in Portuguese.

"JULISSA" IN EL SHOW DE TERROR DE ROCKY (ORIGINAL MEXICAN CAST ALBUM)

* MEXICO 1976 Orfeon Records, LP-13-2277 LP
  Notes: back cover is stamped "NECHO EN MEXICO" Recorded in February 1976. "estereo".

ROCKY HORROR SHOW: NORSK VERSION
(Original Norwegian Cast Album)

* NORWAY 1977 En Talent Produksjon, TLS 3032 LP
  Notes: recorded in Oslo in October 197. There were 2 different print runs of the LP jacket – one came out on thick cardboard stock while the other was printed on very flimsy stock, (however the vinyl is the exact same pressing). Vinyl groove etching on Side 1 & 2: "Roky".

THE ROCKY HORROR SHOW featuring GARY GLITTER
(Original New Zealand Cast Album)
* NEW ZEALAND 1978 Stetson Records Ltd, SRLP 6 white label test pressing LP
  Notes: label is completely white containing no printed information at all.

* NEW ZEALAND 1978 Stetson Records Ltd, SRLP 6 LP
  Notes: Recorded July 31-August 2, 1978. Front cover artwork image of Frank is not actually Gary Glitter but in fact Max Phipps from the 1975 Melbourne, Australian production!

GARY GLITTER WITH THE ROCKY HORRORS
* NEW ZEALAND 1978 Stetson Records Ltd, SP13 demonstrational 7" generic sleeve
  Sweet Transvestite / I'm Going Home 45rpm, stereo
  Notes: demo sticker on label.

* NEW ZEALAND 1978 Stetson Records Ltd, SP13 7", generic sleeve
  Sweet Transvestite / I'm Going Home 45rpm, stereo

PAUL JOHNSTONE WITH THE ROCKY HORRORS
* NEW ZEALAND 1978 Stetson Records Ltd, SP14 demonstrational 7", generic sleeve
  Hot Patootie (Bless My Soul) / Eddie's Teddy 45rpm, stereo
  Notes: demo sticker on label.

* NEW ZEALAND 1978 Stetson Records Ltd, SP14 7", generic sleeve,
  Hot Patootie (Bless My Soul) / Eddie's Teddy 45rpm, stereo
  Notes: demo sticker on label.

ROCKY HORROR SHOW ORIGINAL NEW ZEALAND CAST
* NEW ZEALAND 1981 Stetson Records Ltd, SP28 demonstrational 7" generic sleeve
  Time Warp / Science Fiction - Double Feature 45rpm, stereo
  Notes: demo sticker on label.

* NEW ZEALAND 1981 Stetson Records Ltd, SP28 7" Generic sleeve
  Time Warp / Science Fiction - Double Feature 45rpm, stereo

DIE ROCKY HORROR SHOW LIVE IN DEUTSCHER SPRACHE
(ORIGINAL GERMAN CAST ALBUM)
* GERMANY 1980 Ariola Records, 202 146-315 promotional LP
  Notes: recorded live on 20 January 1980. Cast photos on front & back of LP jacket. Insert sleeve includes complete lyrics in German.

* GERMANY 1980 Ariola Records, 202 146-315 LP
  Notes: recorded live on 20 January 1980. Cast photos on front & back of LP jacket. Insert sleeve includes complete lyrics in German.

THE STEINWAY PIANOLA MEETS ROCKY HORROR
* USA 1980 Recorded Publications Company/ LDH Records, RH603 LP
  Notes: unique interpretation of the RHS musical score on a 1912 Steinway Grand Pianola Piano. Described on the jacket as "A Player-Piano transcription of the stage and film musical The Rocky Horror Show, by Richard O'Brien". Music roll arrangements interpreted by L Douglas Henderson in 1979. Also includes 4 page extensive 'listener notes' written in January 1980 by Henderson.

ALIVE: THE ROCKY HORROR SHOW (1981 AUSTRALIAN REVIVAL CAST EP)
* AUSTRALIA 1981 Festival Records, L20009 promotional red vinyl "MINI LP"
  Notes: promo sticker on front. Released in a clear plastic record cover with double-sided cover insert.

* AUSTRALIA 1981 Festival Records, L20009 red vinyl "MINI LP"
  Notes: released in a clear plastic record cover with double-sided cover insert.

- AUSTRALIA 1989 Festival Records, L20009 black vinyl "MINI LP"
  Notes: released in a plain black cover which also contained the original insert sleeve: This was re-pressed here for the first time on black vinyl for inclusion in The Rocky Horror [Australian] Box Set (1989 Festival Records, L80891/4).

RICHARD O'BRIEN'S THE ROCKY HORROR SHOW: THE WHOLE GORY STORY (1990 LONDON REVIVAL CAST ALBUM)

- UK 1990 Chrysalis Records, CHR 1811 double LP, gatefold cover
  Notes: complete studio recording of the entire stage show, cast photos on gatefold with lyric inserts. With this production, the title of the show was altered to "Richard O'Brien's The Rocky Horror Show". Incidentally, almost all future recordings, tours and new merchandise have since adopted this new 'official' title.

ANTHONY HEAD – SWEET TRANSVESTITE

- UK 1991 Chrysalis Records, CHS 123684 7" PS
  Sweet Transvestite (The Sausage Mix) (6:00) / Sweet Transvestite (Hot-Dog Mix) (3:30)
  Sweet Transvestite (Longer Version) (4:17) / The Time Warp (3:22) 45rpm, stereo
  Notes: this version of The Time Warp is lifted from "The Whole Gory Story" album, however all versions of Sweet Transvestite were re-recorded by Anthony Head when he succeeded the role from Tim McInnerny.

- UK 1991 Chrysalis Records, CHS 3684 promotional 7" PS
  Sweet Transvestite (3:30) / The Time Warp (3:22) 45rpm, stereo
  Notes: cover contains a round white promo sticker with release date stamped inside circle (04 MAR 1991). Also includes an Anthony Head "Chrysalis Records" press information insert sheet.

- UK 1991 Chrysalis Records, CHS 3684 7" PS
  Sweet Transvestite (3:30) / The Time Warp (3:22) 45rpm, stereo

- UK 1991 Chrysalis Records, CHSP 3684 promotional PS 7"
  UNCUT PICTURE DISC, Sweet Transvestite (3:30) / The Time Warp (3:22) 45rpm, stereo
  Notes: still in tact round vinyl not yet cut into Frank shape. Packaged in a clear plastic sleeve with bonus backing cover insert.

ROCKY HORROR EFTIR RICHARD O'BRIEN Í FLUTNINGI LEIKFÉLAGS MH (1991 ORIGINAL ICELANDIC CAST)

- ICELAND 1991 PS MÚSIK, PS91011 LP
  Notes: Limited Edition vinyl pressing released in March 1991 Insert sleeve features cast photos from the production & includes complete lyrics in Icelandic.

THE NEW ROCKY HORROR SHOW (1992 AUSTRALIAN CAST ALBUM)

- AUSTRALIA 1992 Columbia / SONY Records SAMP 454 promotional 12", generic black sleeve
  The New Time Warp (Extended Version) / The New Time Warp / Over At The Frankenstein Place, 45rpm, stereo
  Notes: the complete 1992 Australian Cast recording and "The New Time Warp" single were issued on CD format only. This 12" sampler was a radio promo issue not intended for commercial release.

RICHARD O'BRIEN'S THE NEW ROCKY HORROR SHOW: 25 YEARS YOUNG (1998 LONDON CAST LIVE RECORDING)

- UK 1998 Damn It Janet Records, DAMJAN1TP 12", generic black sleeve
  The Time Warp Face Off 12" Mix (6:14) / The Time Warp Wand 7" Mix (Version 1) (4:32)
  The Time Warp Wand 12" Mix (7:49) 33 1/3rpm, stereo,
  Notes: 'Wand' remixes by Paul Masterson. Vinyl scratching on side B: "NEIL MASTERPIECE" The original version of this track was only available on the 1998 London Cast Live CD recording which did not receive a vinyl release.

- HOLLAND 1998 3MV:NL1201860 12", generic black sleeve
  The Time Warp Face Off 12" Mix (6:14) / The Time Warp Wand 7" Mix (Version 1) (4:32)
  The Time Warp Wand 12" Mix (7:49) 33 1/3rpm, stereo
  Notes: 'Wand' remixes by Paul Masterson.

THE ROCKY HORROR PICTURE SHOW

THE ROCKY HORROR PICTURE SHOW ORIGINAL SOUNDTRACK

- UK 1975 Ode Records, 78332 white label promotional LP
  Notes: record bears completely white label devoid of artwork.

- UK 1975 Ode Records, 78332 LP
  Notes: features black inner record label devoid of artwork.

- UK 1975 Ode Records, 78332 LP
  Notes: label bears silver and white "Ode" logo artwork.

- AUSTRALIA 1975 Ode/ Festival Records, L-35,698 LP
  Notes: disc bears white label featuring "Ode Records" logo.

- CANADA 1975 Ode / A&M Records, Canada SP-77031 promotional LP
  Notes: label bears silver and white "Ode" logo artwork, "Promotion Copy" printed on inner label.

- CANADA 1975 Ode / A&M Records, Canada SP-77031 UN-PRESSED LP
  Notes: blank vinyl record prior to pressing - containing no audio tracks. Label bears RHPS trademark lips and logo.

- THE ROCKY HORROR PICTURE SHOW SOUNDTRACK
  FRANCE 1975 Ode / A&M Records, 875 059 LP
  Notes: Test Pressing. Label is blank white. Comes in stock RHPS sleeve. Printed in France.

- THE ROCKY HORROR PICTURE SHOW ORIGINAL SOUNTRACK
  US 2014 Ode Records ODE-00001-1
  Notes: Exclusive Release by Newbury Comics on translucent vinyl with red streaks.

- CANADA 1975 Ode / A&M Records, Canada SP-77031 LP
  Notes: label bears RHPS trademark lips and logo.

- CANADA 1975 Epic Records, 21653 LP
  Notes: label features 'open' Roxy Trixie lips and logo

- NEW ZEALAND 1975 Ode / Festival Records, L 35304 LP
  Notes: label is blue and bears" Festival" logo artwork

- FRANCE 1975 Ode / A&M Records, 875 059 LP
  Notes: label bears traditional "A&M" style logo artwork (similar to those on all Tim Curry LPs). Inner label also reads "Bande Originale Du Film The Rocky Horror Show" and claims the recording is in BOTH Mono & Stereo which is incorrect. Printed in France.

- GERMANY 1975 Ode Records, 19530 LP
  Notes: label bears silver and white "Ode" logo artwork.

- SOUTH AFRICA 1976 Interpak / Ode Records, AMLS 678332 LP
  Notes: pressed on very thick vinyl, disc bears white label featuring silver "Ode" logo

- JAPAN 1976 King Records, FML-54 LP
  Notes: contains obi strip and insert.

- JAPAN 1976 CBS-Sony, 25AP 59 promotional LP
  Notes: contains obi strip. "Sample" stamped on label.

- SOUTH AFRICA 1977 Epic Records, KSF 2007 LP
  Notes: label bears generic purple "Epic" logo artwork.

- SOUTH AFRICA 1977 Epic Records, COL 40077 LP
  Notes: label bears generic purple "Epic" logo artwork. Round black "Star Spectacular Original Artists" sticker on cover sleeve.

- USA 1978 Ode Records, OSV21653 LP
  Notes: First US pressing, label bears RHPS trademark lips and logo.

- USA 1978 Ode Records, SP-77031 LP
  Notes: label features 'open' Roxy Trixie lips and logo.

- USA 1978 Ode Records, 77031 LP
  Notes: re-issue includes RHPS Official Fan Club application flyer, label features RHPS trademark lips and logo

- UK 1986 Ode/Pacific Records, LP: OSV 21653 LP
  Notes: re-issue of 1975 original; label features RHPS trademark lips and logo.

- AUSTRALIA 1987 Festival Records, L-35698 LP
  Notes: re-issue of 1975 original; label features RHPS trademark lips and logo.

- USA 1989 Rainbo Records, S-R116-70089 white label test pressing LP
  Notes: test pressing made by Rainbo for Rhino Records. Contains a "Rainbo Test pressing" label with date and the word "Rhino" handwritten.

- USA 1989 Rhino Records, Rhino -R170712, LP
  Notes: label features RHPS trademark lips and logo.

- ITALY 1989 Greenline Records, GRP 3314 LP
  Notes: record contains white inner label featuring RHPS lips and album information printed in green ink

- UK 2002 Castle Music/ Sanctuary Records, CMHLP474 LP
  Notes: re-released as a companion piece to the new Castle Records CD issue in "miniature" LP sleeve packaging design. Label features RHPS trademark lips and logo.

- GERMANY 2002 Castle Music, CASTL:0159147410 LP
  Notes: re-released as a companion piece to the new Castle Records CD issue in "miniature" LP sleeve packaging design. Label features RHPS trademark lips and logo.

- HOLLAND 2002 Castle Music, CASTL:847858 LP
  Notes: re-released as a companion piece to the new Castle Records CD issue in "miniature" LP sleeve packaging design. Label features RHPS trademark lips and logo.

- USA 2004 Earmark Records, EAR 420381 LP
  Notes: re-issue of 1975 original; Contains a round black "Earmark 180 gram virgin vinyl" sticker on the cover sleeve.

THE ROCKY HORROR PICTURE SHOW
ORIGINAL SOUNDTRACK (Red Vinyl)

- AUSTRALIA 1978 Festival Records, L35698 LP, *bright* red vinyl
  Notes: cover features a large round sticker stating "Collector's Item Limited Edition Red Vinyl" This special edition was produced in Australia in 1978 to celebrate the extraordinary achievement of the Original Movie Soundtrack exceeding sales of 10,000 copies per week!

- AUSTRALIA 1981 Festival Records, L35698 LP, *bright* red vinyl
  Notes: cover features a large round sticker stating "Limited Edition Colored Vinyl Collector's Item" This second special edition was produced in Australia in 1981 to celebrate the first Australian National revival of the stage show (and was initially offered as a companion to the 1981 Australian Revival Cast EP - also pressed on stunning red vinyl).

- AUSTRALIA 1981 Festival Records, L35698 promotional *dark* red vinyl LP
  Notes: this alternate promo pressing was not available for purchase and features no round sticker on the cover. Pressed on a different, much darker, shade of red vinyl and likewise released to celebrate the first Australian National revival of the stage show (however only offered to radio stations and exclusive record stores).

- USA 2013 Ode Records / The Orchard, ODE-00001-1 LP, translucent red vinyl
  Notes: Limited edition re-issue of 1975 original on bright transparent red vinyl. Contains a square black sticker on cover stating "The original soundtrack from the #1 Cult Movie of All Time Now on Red vinyl!".

THE ROCKY HORROR PICTURE SHOW ORIGINAL SOUNDTRACK (US PICTURE DISC)

- USA 1979 Ode Records, OPD 91653 picture disc LP, "Limited Edition"
  Notes: first pressing of the picture disc individually numbered. Pressed onto each side, are 2 images of Tim Curry as Frank from the 1974 Roxy production photo shoot. Vinyl picture is completely visible through a cut out section in the front of the jacket.

- USA 1979 Ode Records, OPD 91653 picture disc LP, "Limited Edition II"
  Notes: second pressing of the picture disc individually numbered. Pressed onto each side, are 2 images of Tim Curry as Frank from the 1974 Roxy production photo shoot. Vinyl picture is completely visible through a cut out section in the front of the jacket.

- USA 1979 Ode / Jem Records Inc, OPD 91653 picture disc LP, "Limited Edition"
  Notes: second issue of the "Limited Edition" picture disc - distributed through Jem Records, New Jersey. Also individually numbered - commencing at higher numbers. Same 2 images of Tim Curry as Frank pressed onto each side.

- USA 1979 Ode /Jem Records Inc, OPD 91653 picture disc LP, "Limited Edition II"
  Notes: second issue of the "Limited Edition II" picture disc - distributed through Jem Records, New Jersey. Also individually numbered - commencing at higher numbers. Same 2 images of Tim Curry as Frank pressed onto each side.

THE ROCKY HORROR PICTURE SHOW ORIGINAL SOUNDTRACK (UK PICTURE DISC)

- UK 1987 Ode/Pacific Records, OSVP 21653 picture disc LP
  Notes UK re-issue of the original 1979 US version, contains similar front picture but a completely different B-side image. It features the cast throne scene and RHPS logo & film credits on a black background. Not released with any cover sleeve jacket, just housed inside a clear plastic record sleeve. Printed artwork on the record labels side 1 with the figure "1" (all other picture discs spell the number as "side one") Very limited run and extremely less common than any of the "Limited Edition" US pressings.

- UK 1987 Ode /Pacific Records, OSVP 21653 picture disc LP
  Notes: scarce Promo version of the UK re-issue (as above). This release has a different image pressed onto the B-side altogether! It features a variation of the graphics seen on the sleeve of the original movie soundtrack. Also includes logo & film credits on a bright red background. The word "the" is omitted from the RHPS title logo. Very limited run and extremely less common than any other picture disc!

20TH CENTURY FOX PRESENTS THE ROCKY HORROR PICTURE SHOW RADIO SPOTS

- USA 1975 20th Century Fox, DS211 promotional 7" Plain sleeve, 331/3rpm, stereo
  Notes: single-sided promotional EP. Contains seven 30 second and one 60 second publicity radio spots performed by Richard O'Brien.

- USA 1975 20th Century Fox, DS211 promotional 7", plain sleeve, 331/3rpm, stereo
  Notes: single-sided promotional EP (as above) however in this pressing the non-playable B-side has a silver label (instead of pink).

SCIENCE FICTION-DOUBLE FEATURE / TIME WARP

- UK 1975 Ode Records, ODS 66305 white label test pressing 7", generic sleeve
  Science Fiction-Double Feature (3:15) / Time Warp (4:30) 45rpm, stereo
  Notes: features plain white label devoid of any printing with 'Rocky Horror' and 'A+M Records' hand written in red on one side. Catalogue number 'ODS 66305 A/B' also hand-written on the paper sleeve.

- UK 1975 Ode Records, ODS 66305 7", generic sleeve,
  Science Fiction-Double Feature (3:15) (The RHPS Original Cast) / Time Warp (4:30) (Richard O'Brien) 45rpm, stereo
  Notes: double "A" side single, disc bears white label featuring silver "Ode" logo. Track lengths on each side are incorrectly switched i.e. Science Fiction should be (4:30).

- SOUTH AFRICA 1976 Ode Records Inc, AMRO 1173 7", generic sleeve,
  Science Fiction-Double Feature (3:15) (Richard O'Brien) / Time Warp (4:30) (Richard O'Brien) 45rpm, stereo
  Notes: Richard O'Brien is credited as the artist on both tracks & his name is misspelled on side one as "O'Brian". Track lengths on each side are incorrectly switched i.e. Science Fiction should be (4:30).

SELECTED SELECTIONS FROM THE ORIGINAL SOUNDTRACK FROM THE ORIGINAL MOVIE

- USA 1975 Ode Records, OSV-21653 7" PS
  Hot Patootie-Bless My Soul / The Time Warp / Touch-A, Touch-A, Touch Me, Sweet Transvestite 45rpm, stereo

THE TIME WARP/HOT PATOOTIE-BLESS MY SOUL

- AUSTRALIA 1976 Interfusion/Festival Records, K7200 7" Generic "Festival Records" sleeve
  The Time Warp (The RHPS Original Cast) / Hot Patootie-Bless My Soul (Meatloaf as Eddie) 45rpm, stereo

- NEW ZEALAND 1978 Interfusion/Festival Records, K7200 7" Generic "Festival Records" sleeve
  The Time Warp (Original Cast) / Hot Patootie-Bless My Soul (Meatloaf as Eddie) 45rpm, stereo

- AUSTRALIA 1978 Interfusion/Festival Records, K7200 7", Generic "Festival Records" sleeve
  The Time Warp (Original Cast) / Hot Patootie-Bless My Soul (Meat Loaf as Eddie) 45rpm, stereo
  Notes: re-pressed in 1980 simply crediting the track to "Original Cast" Entered the Australian Top 40 singles charts (peeking at #2 in July 1980!).

- AUSTRALIA 1991 Interfusion/Festival Records, K10414 7" Generic "Festival Records" sleeve
  The Time Warp (Soundtrack Original Cast) / Hot Patootie-Bless My Soul (Soundtrack Meat Loaf as Eddie) 45rpm, stereo
  Notes: third issue by Festival in conjunction with the re-release of the RHPS on video cassette. Also released on 'cassingle'.

- USA 1978 Prime Records, PRM-78-10 jukebox 10" Generic sleeve
  The Time Warp (3:15) (Riff Raff, Columbia Magenta and The Transylvanians)
  Hot Patootie-Bless My Soul (3:00) (Eddie) 78rpm, stereo
  Notes: unique jukebox 10" single which plays at 78rpm!

SWEET TRANSVESTITE/ SCIENCE FICTION-DOUBLE FEATURE

- AUSTRALIA 1981 Festival Records/ Interfusion, K-8246 7" Generic "Festival Records" sleeve
  Sweet Transvestite (3:21) (The RHPS Original Cast) / Science Fiction-Double Feature (1:28) (The RHPS Original Cast) 45rpm, stereo
  Notes: Side B lists the song as "Science Fiction-Double Feature" when it is actually "Science Fiction-Double Feature (Reprise)" Released in April, 1981.

- NEW ZEALAND 1981 Interfusion Records, K-8246 7" Generic "Interfusion" sleeve
  Sweet Transvestite (3:21) (The RHPS Original Cast) / Science Fiction-Double Feature (1:28) (The RHPS Original Cast) 45rpm, stereo
  Notes: Side B lists the song as "Science Fiction-Double Feature" when it is actually "Science Fiction-Double Feature (Reprise)".

THE TIME WARP / SWEET TRANSVESTITE

- CANADA 1975 Epic Records, E4-8424 7" Generic "Epic Records" sleeve
  The Time Warp (Riff Raff, Columbia Magenta And The Transylvanians) / Sweet Transvestite (Frank N Furter from The ODE Epic LP "Rocky Horror Picture Show") 45rpm, stereo
  Notes: Cut-out jukebox hole.

- CANADA 1975 Epic Records, E4-8424 promo 7" Generic "Epic Records" sleeve
  The Time Warp (mono) / The Time Warp (stereo) 45rpm, mono/stereo
  Notes: Cut-out jukebox hole.

THE TIME WARP - ORIGINAL FILM SOUNDTRACK ORIGINAL ROXY CAST

*   USA 1986 ODE Records Inc, PRCC-11 promotional split 7" Generic sleeve
    The Time Warp (Roxy Cast) (3:57) / The Time Warp (Film Soundtrack) (3:15) 45rpm, stereo
    Notes: Cut-out jukebox hole, catalogue number etched into vinyl.

THE TIME WARP REMIX 1989

*   USA 1989 Ode/ Rhino Records, RNTW 70411 12" PS
    The Time Warp 1989 Remix Extended Version (5:35) / The Time Warp Remix 1989 Version (4:12) The Time Warp-Music-1=
    Background + U Mix (4:08) 33 1/3rpm, stereo
    Notes: all mixes are previously unreleased tracks.

TIME WARP -THE ROCKY HORROR PICTURE SHOW ORIGINAL SOUNDTRACK

*   USA 2003 Erika Records, (no catalogue number) 10" picture disc
    Time Warp / Sweet Transvestite Notes Limited Edition exclusive release for Hot Topic stores

RHPS SOUNDTRACK RELATED RELEASES

THE ENTIRE ROCKY HORROR PICTURE SHOW (Bootleg Album)

*   USA 1978 - white label double bootleg LP
    Notes: Contains no label or catalogue number. Poor quality MONO recording of the film, back of jacket is plain white. Front cover features a hand drawn cartoon image of Frank and has the following printed: "All the songs! All the dialogue! The Entire Rocky Horror Picture Show! Now You Can Hear: Planet Shmanet Janet, Sword of Damocles, Transylvanian Jam Session, Super Heroes-And ALL the sounds of the Frank N. Furter Castle!".

THE ROCKY HORROR PICTURE SHOW AUDIENCE PARTIC-I-PATION ALBUM

*   USA 1983 Ode Records, ODE 1032 double LP, gatefold cover
    Notes: recorded live at the 8th Street Playhouse, New York. Master of Ceremonies, Special Consultant & additional material compiled by Sal Piro. Insert sleeves contain partial Audience Participation script with call back lines. Also printed is the "Official" RHPS Prop List, and a guide to Rocky Horror Etiquette.

*   AUSTRALIA 1983 Ode / Festival Records, L70231/2 double LP, gatefold cover
    Notes: Australian release as above. Sound audio matches the original MONO version of the movie.

*   NEW ZEALAND 1983 Festival / Interfusion Records - L70231/2 double LP Gatefold cover
    Notes: New Zealand release as above. Sound audio matches the original MONO version of the movie.

*   CANADA 1983 Ode / CBS Records Ltd ODE 90706 double LP, gatefold cover
    Notes: featuring new text in blue added to front cover artwork: "The Original Soundtrack To The Original Soundtrack From The Original Movie" Insert sleeves contain partial Participation script with call back lines. Sound audio matches the original MONO version of the movie! Inner label does not feature RHPS lips/logo artwork.

*   UK 1983 Ode Records, ODE 1032 double LP, gatefold cover,
    Notes: no text on cover.

*   UK 1983 Ode Records, ODE 1032 double LP, gatefold cover
    Notes: re-issue with text on cover.Lips and logo printed on record labels.

*   UK 1987 Ode Records, ODE 1032 double LP, gatefold cover
    Notes: first UK release featuring new text in white added to front cover artwork: "The Original Soundtrack To The Original Soundtrack From The Original Movie" Insert sleeves contain partial Participation script with call back lines. Sound audio matches the original MONO version of the movie.

*   AUSTRALIA 1987 Ode / Festival Records L70231/2 double LP, gatefold cover
    Notes: re-issue featuring new text in white added to front cover: "The Original Soundtrack To The Original Soundtrack From The Original Movie" Insert sleeves contain partial Participation script with call back lines. Sound audio matches the original MONO version of the movie.

- CANADA 1987 Ode / CBS Records Ltd ODE 90706 double LP, gatefold cover
  Notes: re-issue featuring new text in blue added to front cover artwork: "The Original Soundtrack To The Original Soundtrack From The Original Movie" Insert sleeves contain partial Participation script with call back lines Sound audio matches the original MONO version of the movie! Inner label does not feature RHPS lips/logo artwork.

- USA 1989 Rainbo Records, S-R116-70089 white label test pressing LP
  Notes: test pressing made by Rainbo for Rhino Records. Label states "Customer:Rhino" followed by "S" and the pressing date "4-12-89"It also contains hand written reference numbers "12-in-71112" and elsewhere "S-21764/65"

- USA 1989 Rhino Records, R1-71112 double LP, gatefold cover
  Notes: US re-issue featuring new text in white added to front cover: "The Original Soundtrack To The Original Soundtrack From The Original Movie" Insert sleeves contain partial Participation script with call back lines. Sound audio matches the original MONO version of the movie!

DMC APRIL 1991 (ROCKY HORROR THE ANTICIPATION/PARTICIPATION MEGAMIX

- UK 1991 DMC Records Limited, APR 91 promotional 12" PS
  Remember The Day by The Unforgettable Fire Innocence * It's Too Late by Quartz Featuring Dina Carroll / ROCKY HORROR - THE ANTICIPATION PARICIPATION MEGAMIX (includes: Sweet Transvestite, Damn It Janet, T-T-T-T-Touch Me, The Time Warp) * Break Beat Of The Month 45rpm, stereo
  Notes: "Not for sale"; these were DJ-only issued remixes available exclusively to club members. Side 2 includes an extended RH remix of tracks taken from the "Audience Participation Album" including dialogue by MC Sal Piro.

THE ROCKY HORROR 20TH ANNIVERSARY FAN TRIBUTE ALBUM

- USA 1995 Krunchy Panties Records, 4711 bootleg LP
  Notes: "A Completely Crazy Production" Limited Edition of 500 copies individually numbered. Unique theatre recording "Of The Fans! By The Fans! For The Fans!" Includes booklet and a 'cassette offer' coupon. Sound levels are incredibly quiet! Vinyl groove etchings: Side A: "4711-A", side B: "4711-B".

- USA 1995 Krunchy Panties Records, 4711 bootleg LP
  Notes: alternate pressing of the above record which is not individually numbered and does not include insert booklet or the 'cassette offer' coupon.

THE ROCKY HORROR PICTURE SHOW ORIGINAL SOUNDTRACK

- AUSTRALIA 1979 Festival Records, L35698 framed Gold LP
  Notes: A framed display piece consisting of a gold record for "The Rocky Horror Picture Show" selling 50,000 units in Australia matted next to the original album jacket and a small commemorative plaque.

- USA 1990 Ode Records, OSV21653 framed Platinum LP
  Notes: A framed display piece consisting of a platinum record for "The Rocky Horror Picture Show" matted next to the original album jacket and a color photograph signed by Meatloaf.

- UK 198? Ode Records, 78332 framed Gold LP
  Notes: A framed display piece consisting of a gold record for " The Rocky Horror Picture Show" selling 500,000 units in the UK matted next to the original album jacket and a small commemorative plaque CERTIFIED RIAA SALES AWARD.

- CANADA 1998 Ode Records / Roy Créations Internationales, OSV21653 Custom framed Gold LP
  Notes: A 28"X 28" framed display piece consisting of a gold plated record for "The Rocky Horror Picture Show" matted next to the original album jacket and a small commemorative plaque. This one of a kind frame was individually hand crafted by renowned gold record artist STEPHANE ROY and is signed with a Certificate of Authenticity & numbered 1/1.

ROCKY HORROR CD's

THE ROCKY HORROR SHOW

- The Rocky Horror Show
  New Australian Cast
  Australia 1992 Columbia Records 472855

- The Rocky Horror Show
  1995 UK Jay Records CDJAY 1299
  Notes: Budget studio cast recording featuring Brian May of Queen as Eddie and many veterans of past and future stage productions of "The Rocky Horror Show".

- The Rocky Horror Show
  1995 "NEW" New Zealand Cast
  1995 New Zealand BMG/Stetson Recordings BMG SRCD 25

- The Rocky Horror Show
  1995 Iclandic Cast Recording
  Iceland 1995 Flugfelagio Loftur FL002
  Notes: All lyrics performed in Icelandic.

- RICHARD O BRIEN'S THE ROCKY HORROR SHOW
  Soundtrack from the European Tour 1996/1997
  UK 1996 Polymedia LV-62814

- THE ROCKY HORROR SHOW
  Bad Hersfeld, Germany cast recording
  Germany 1997 Multi Culture Records LC 3286
  Notes: all songs sung in English.

- THE NEW ROCKY HORROR SHOW: 25 years young
  UK 1998 Damn It Janet Records DAMJAN2CD
  Notes: New cast recording featuring Jason Donovan as Frank.

- UK 2008 Metro Records
  Notes: Re-release of the 1998 recording with different artwork

- THE TIME WARP
  UK 1998 Damn It Janet Records DAMJAN1CD   Cd Single
  Notes: Contains 3 Different mixes of "The Time Warp".

- RICHARD O BRIEN'S THE ROCKY HORROR SHOW
  Broadway Revival Cast Recording
  2001 RCA Victor 09026-63801-2

- RICHARD O BRIEN'S THE ROCKY HORROR SHOW
  Korean Cast Recording
  Korea 2001 BMG ENEC-018
  Notes: with the exception of "Science Fiction Double Feature" all lyrics are in Korean.

- RICHARD O BRIENS' THE ROCKY HORROR SHOW
  The Vancouver Cast Recording
  Canada 2005 No Label (Private Release)

- THE ROCKY HORROR GLEE SHOW
  US 2010 Columbia Records 88697 79646 2 EP
  Notes: Studio recordings from the special Halloween episode of the TV show "Glee".

LP BOX SETS

THE ROCKY HORROR ('SAY IT!') BOX SET
- UK 1988 Pacific Records, RHBX1 3xLP boxed set, (contains The RHS 1974 Original Roxy Cast LP, The Rocky Horror Picture Show Original Soundtrack LP, & The RHPS Audience Partic-i-pation double LP).

Notes: Limited Edition, individually numbered. Box cover has gold embossing. Also contains bonus folded poster of Tim Curry as Frank (famous Roxy pose) & 2 "Say It!" buttons. This was the first ever RH box set and was limited to 5,000 copies. Initially filled with 'surprise' loose confetti!

THE ROCKY HORROR SHOW ALBUM BOX SET

* UK 1988 Pacific Records, RHBXLP1 3xLP boxed set, (contains The RHS 1974 Original Roxy Cast LP, The Rocky Horror Picture Show Original Soundtrack LP, & The RHPS Audience Partic-i-pation double LP).
Notes: Also includes Time Warp dance steps sheet, the RHPS Official Fan Club membership form, and a 15 page RHPS photo/lyric booklet. This was a repackaged version of the original Limited Edition Box Set. Cover art features RHPS cast throne scene.

THE ROCKY HORROR BOX SET

* AUSTRALIA 1989 Festival Records, L80891/4 4xLP boxed set, (contains The Original 1974 Australian Cast LP, The Rocky Horror Picture Show Original Soundtrack LP, 1981 Australian Revival Cast "Alive" Tour EP & The RHPS Audience Partic-i-pation double LP)
Notes: also included a promotional Shock Treatment "Cosmo McKinley" face mask and a Rocky Horror lips sticker. This was only available for a very limited time! The 1981 Australian Revival Cast EP (originally released on RED vinyl) was pressed for the first time on regular black vinyl for inclusion in this box set! Also, there were 5 different versions of the promotional Cosmo masks (Each had a different message printed on the back including: "The Rocky Horror Gang", "Brad And Janet Are Back", "Trust Me I'm A Doctor", "Original Soundtrack on Records And Tapes" & "Be A Real Live Wire" Initially filled with 'surprise' loose confetti!

SHOCK TREATMENT

SHOCK TREATMENT ORIGINAL FILM SOUNDTRACK

* UK 1981 Warner Brothers Records, WBK56957 promotional LP

* UK 1981 Warner Brothers Records, WBK56957 LP

* USA 1981 Warner Brothers Records Inc, LLA 3615 promotional LP, *Notes: gold Stamped promo*

* USA 1981 Warner Brothers Records Inc, LLA 3615 LP
Notes: sticker on cover reads: "From The Creators of the Rocky Horror Picture Show - The Continuing Adventures Of Brad, Janet and Richard O'Brien".

* USA 1981 Warner Brothers Records Inc, OSV 21654 (LLA 3615) LP
Notes: standard US issue as above but with a sticker on cover replacing the old cat# with "OVS 21654" (which is also pasted over spine). JEM records DJ sticker on front as well as custom sticker stating "from the creators of the Rocky Horror Picture Show, the continuing adventures of Brad, Janet and Richard O'Brien".

* CANADA 1981 Warner Bros, XLA 3615 LP

* AUSTRALIA 1981 Interfusion/Festival Records, L 37716 LP
Notes: original pressing, cover features a Limited Edition promo sticker offer: "Includes bonus cut out mask of Cosmo Mckinley" Also contained a double-sided Rocky Horror 'Festival Records' soundtrack promotional flyer.

* AUSTRALIA 1981 Interfusion/Festival Records, L 37716 LP
Notes: second pressing - does not contain Cosmo promo adhesive sticker or the bonus mask/flyer.

* PORTUGAL 1981 Warner Brothers Records, WAR56957 LP

* NEW ZEALAND 1981 Festival / Interfusion Records, L 37716 LP

* GERMANY 1981 Warner Brothers Records, WB K56957 LP

* SPAIN 1981 Hispavox Warner, S 90 490 LP

* SOUTH AFRICA 1981 Warner Brothers Records, 1517 LP

* ITALY 1983 Warner Bros. Records Inc/Wea Italiana S.P.A Milano, W 56957 LP
  Notes: cover features a printed yellow circle stating "THE ROCKY HORROR PICTURE SHOW n.2", vinyl groove etching gives release date as 28/2/83.

SHOCK TREATMENT – RICHARD O'BRIEN

* USA 1981 Warner Brothers Records Inc, PRO-A-976 promotional white label 12" PS
  Shock Treatment (2:49) / Overture (2:16) 45rpm, stereo
  Notes: cuts taken from "The Lou Adler/Michael White Production Of A New Musical By Richard O'Brien SHOCK TREATMENT" Label reads "Promotional Copy. Not For Sale" Spine of jacket incorrectly labelled as "Shock Treatment Original Sound Track.".

* UK 1981 Warner Brothers Records, K.17882 promotional 7" PS, Shock Treatment (2:49) / Overture (2:16) 45rpm, stereo

* USA 1981 Warner Brothers Records Inc, LAS 49799 test pressing 7" PS
  Shock Treatment (2:49) / Overture (2:16) 45rpm, stereo
  Notes: white label test pressing devoid of artwork. label states: "Promo Not For Sale" written in marker pen "SHOCK TREATMENT" AND "RICHARD O'BRIEN" label is all white and reads PROMO NOT FOR SALE - SIDE B - AS-49799 – no one has written anything on the B side, Jukebox cut out hole.

* USA 1981 Warner Brothers Records Inc, LAS 49799 promotional 7" PS
  Shock Treatment (2:49) / Overture (2:16) 45rpm, stereo
  Notes: inner label states: "Promotional. Not For Sale" Jukebox cut out hole.

* USA 1981 Warner Brothers Records Inc, LAS 49799 7" PS, Shock Treatment (2:49) / Overture (2:16) 45rpm, stereo
  Notes: Jukebox cut out hole.

SHOCK TREATMENT – RICHARD O'BRIEN NELL CAMPBELL PATRICIA QUINN

* AUSTRALIA 1981 Interfusion/Festival Records, K 8548 red vinyl 7" PS
  Shock Treatment (2:15) / Overture (2:16) 45rpm, stereo
  Notes:" limited edition release" printed on cover.

* AUSTRALIA 1981 Interfusion/Festival Records, K 8548 black vinyl 7" PS
  Shock Treatment (2:15) / Overture (2:16) 45rpm, stereo
  Notes: The UK & USA releases both feature Richard O'Brien's solo remixed version of "Shock Treatment" (i.e. the version following the film's end credits). The Australian release contains the standard original soundtrack recording and adds "Nell Campbell" & "Patricia Quinn" to the front sleeve under the title.

MISCELLANEOUS ROCKY HORROR COVERS

THE LIFE ORGANISATION - TIME WARP FROM THE ROCKY HORROR SHOW

* AUSTRALIA 1974 Polydor Records, 2079-045 7", generic "Polydor" sleeve
  Time Warp / The Sweet Song, 45rpm
  Notes: early cover versions produced by Tony Barber and William Moltzing. "Sweet Transvestite" is retitled "The Sweet Song" with all references in the chorus to transvestism removed.

THE MISFITS

* DeA.D. AliveUS 2013 Misfits Records MRLP 01550 LP
  Notes: released on Gold Opaque vinyl limited to 1500 and Gold with red and white splitter vinyl limited to 500. Contains their live recording of "Science Fiction Double Feature".

- Descending Angel/Science Fiction Double Feature
  US 2013 Misfits Records MLRP 01570 12"Single PS
  Notes: Released on Clear vinyl with black and white splatter (500 copies), white vinyl with black splatter(300 copies), Clear vinyl with black and red splatter (500 copies), and regular black vinyl. Contains their studio recording of "Science Fiction/Double Feature". Back Sleeve photography by Mick Rock.

PETER STRAKER - TOUCH ME

- UK 1975 Pye Records, 7N 45486 7", generic "Pye" sleeve
  Touch Me (mono) / Touch Me (stereo) 45rpm, stereo/mono
  Notes: Peter Straker was a notorious '70s glam rock star & stage actor. He was also a musical collaborator with Freddie Mercury of Queen.

- UK 1975 Pye Records, 7N 45486 7", generic "Pye" sleeve
  Touch Me (4:00) / We Had It All 45rpm,
  Notes: Richard O'Brien's writing credit is misspelled as "Richard O'Brian". Produced by Don Fraser.

JUST US GIRLS - TIME WARP

- USA 1979 Epic/Cleveland International Records, 8-50733 promotional 7", generic sleeve
  Time Warp (stereo) (3:45) / Time Warp (mono) (3:45) 45rpm, stereo/mono
  Notes: label states "Demonstration Not For Sale" produced by Dick Wagner and Michael Kamen for Mother Fortune Inc. jukebox cut-out hole.

- USA 1979 Epic/Cleveland International Records, 8-50733 promotional 7", generic sleeve
  Time Warp (3:45) / By The Fire (1:59) 45rpm, stereo
  Notes: produced by Dick Wagner and Michael Kamen for Mother Fortune Inc.

- USA 1979 Epic/Cleveland International Records, AS 626 promotional 12", generic sleeve
  Time Warp (5:41) / By The Fire (1:59) 33 1/3rpm, stereo
  Notes: produced by Dick Wagner and Michael Kamen for Mother Fortune Inc.

20 ROCK MUSICAL GREATS

- UK 1977 Arcade Records ADE P31
  Notes: Contains a cover of "Sweet Transvestite". This seems to be one of those bargain LP's where a studio band does covers of popular songs.

VINCE VANCE AND THE VALIANTS - DOUBLE ALUMINUM

- 1977 ICA Records (No Catalog Number)
  Notes: comes in a plain white cardboard sleeve. Contains a live cover of "Hot Patootie".

LOU AND THE HOLLYWOOD BANANAS – TROISIEME DIMENSION (TIME WARP)

- FRANCE 1981 RKM Records/Disques Vogue, 101490 7", PS
  Troisieme dimension (Time Warp) (3:13) / Si t' etais dans mes chaussures (3:27) 45rpm, stereo
  Notes: sung entirely in French and includes lyrics for Time Warp printed in French on back of sleeve, jukebox cut-out hole. Lyrics adapted into Francaise by Michel Moers.

- Spain 1981 Hispa/Vox Records 45-2176 7"single PS
  Deforma El Tiempo Otra Vez (Time Warp)/Pes Peur Du Loup (Big Bad Wolf
  Notes: Spanish language cover of "Time Warp". Back of picture sleeve features lyrics in Spanish.

- TIMBIRICHE
  1983 Melody Records PE-4109 7"Single Promo
  Baile Del Sapo (Time Warp)/Baile Del Sapo (Time Warp)
  Notes: Spanish language cover of "Time Warp"" by a popular Mexican teen group from the 80's. Julissa, who translated and starred in the first Mexican production of The Rocky Horror Show, was the mother of one of the teens in this group.

- FRANCE 1981 RKM Records/Vogue, 101491 7" PS
  Time Warp (3:13) / Big Bad Wolf (4:03) 45rpm, stereo
  Notes: Second French issue sung in English & includes lyrics for Time Warp printed in English on back of sleeve, jukebox cut-out hole.

- GERMANY 1981 RKM/Hansa International, 103 234 promotional 7", generic sleeve
  Time Warp (stereo) (3:12) / Time Warp (mono) (3:12) 45rpm, stereo
  Notes: Recorded in English.

- GERMANY 1981 RKM/Hansa International, 103 234 7" PS
  Time Warp (3:12) / Big Bad Wolf (4:03) 45rpm, stereo
  Notes: Recorded in English & includes lyrics for Time Warp printed on back of sleeve, jukebox cut-out hole.

- PORTUGAL 1981 RKM Records, 006 7", PS
  Time Warp (3:12) / Big Bad Wolf (4:03) 45rpm, stereo
  Notes: Recorded in English issued in same sleeve as the German release with lyrics for Time Warp printed on back, jukebox cut-out hole.

LOU AND THE HOLLYWOOD BANANAS – S/T
- FRANCE 1981 RKM Records, 520379 LP,
  Notes: self-titled album which includes the group's English cover version of Time Warp.

MINA - SWEET TRANSVESTITE
- ITALY 1982 PDU Records, PAJB 151 promotional 7", generic sleeve
  Mi Piace Tanto La Gente / Sweet Transvestite 45rpm, stereo
  Notes: side 2 contains her English cover version of Sweet Transvestite, jukebox cut out hole.

- ITALY 1982 PDU Records, PAJB 151 promotional 7", generic sleeve
  Sweet Transvestite (mono) / Sweet Transvestite (stereo) 45rpm,
  Notes: promo release of Sweet Transvestite however it was only officially released as a b-side to "Mi Piace Tanto La Gente", *jukebox cut out hole.*

MINA ITALIANA VOL 2
- ITALY 1982 PDU Records, PLD7033 LP
  Notes: 9 track 'Best Of' compilation which includes track 2 - her English cover version of Sweet Transvestite.

TIMBIRICHE - BAILE DEL SAPO (TIME WARP)
- MEXICO 1983 TPE-6738 7", generic sleeve, Baile del Sapo / ?? 45rpm, stereo

LA BANDA TIMBIRICHE
- *MEXICO 1983 LP*
  Notes: includes "Baile del Sapo" – the group's Spanish cover version of Time Warp.

LA BANDA TIMBIRICHE EN CONCIERTO
- *MEXICO 1983 LP*
  Notes: includes "Baile del Sapo" – the group's Spanish cover version of Time Warp live in concert

DEBRIA BROWN - TOUCH ME
- AUSTRIA 1984 Phillips Records, 818 506-7 7" PS
  Touch Me / Touch Me (Instrumental) 45rpm, stereo
  Notes: Recorded in Austria during the 1984 stage production. Cover states: "aus der Rocky Horror Picture Show in der Produktion des Schauspielhaus Wien".

SYUSY BLADY
- Italy 1987 Polydor Records 885 841-7 PS
  Ninna Nanna Yeeeeh! 4:23/Tocca, Toccami 3:24
  Notes: Italian "Disco" cover of "Touch-a Touch Me".

DAVID & ROXANA - THE ROCKY HORROR DISCO SHOW
* GERMANY 1985 ZYX Records, ZYX 5299 promotional 12" PS
  Vocal Version (9:02) /.Instrumental Version (8:49) 45rpm, stereo
  Notes: Recorded at B.M.S "Santanna Studios" Italy. Produced by Cruisin Records, Italy. Lead Vocals by David and Roxana. Promo stamp on back cover and printed on inner label.

* *GERMANY 1985 ZYX Records, ZYX 5299 12" PS*
  Vocal Version (9:02) /.Instrumental Version (8:49) 45rpm, stereo
  Notes: Recorded at B.M.S "Santanna Studios" Italy. Produced by Cruisin Records, Italy. Lead Vocals by David and Roxana.

RUMBLE ON THE BEACH - TIME WARP / "RUMBLE" EP
* GERMANY 1988 Vielklang, EFA 04244-80 LP
  Notes: 7 track EP including their English cover version of Time Warp (3:30) on side 2 (Written by Richard O'Brien), stereo.

FORGOTTON REBELS - SCIENCE FICTION-DOUBLE FEATURE / "SURFIN' ON HEROIN" LP
* USA 1988 Restless Records, 72357 LP
  Notes: includes their cover of "Science Fiction Double Feature (Theme from The Rocky Horror Show)" (5:45).

* CANADA 1988 Star Records, SR 1846 LP
  Notes: includes their cover of "Science Fiction Double Feature (Theme from The Rocky Horror Show)" (5:45).

WARP MACHINE - TIME WARP
* GERMANY 1995 EFA/Franky's Music International, MS 10161-6 12", plain black sleeve
  Time Warp (Radio Edit) (3:38) Time Warp (Extended Version) (4:47) /
  Time Warp (A Capella Edit) (2:32) Time Warp (Instrumental Mix) (4:41) 45rpm, stereo
  Notes: techno cover version dance mixes. Vocals performed by Annika Klar, Jan Lipfert, Andreas Fischer & Thomas Pohl.

BURNIN' GROOVE - TIME WARP
* USA 1996 Incubator Records, 100307 red vinyl 7" PS
  Anybody See / Time Warp 45rpm, stereo
  Notes: cover states "Limited Edition Burnin' Red Vinyl".

ME FIRST AND THE GIMMIE GIMMIES - SCIENCE FICTION / "ARE A DRAG" LP
* USA 1999 Fat Wreck Chords, FAT 586-1 LP
  Notes: includes their cover of "Science-Fiction", lyric sheet included.

* HOLLAND 1999 Sonic Rend, 314811 LP
  Notes: includes their cover of "Science-Fiction".

* GERMANY 1999 Fat Wreck Chords, 676559 LP
  Notes: includes their cover of "Science-Fiction".

SWINGIN' UTTERS -- EDDIE / "SWINGIN' UTTERS" LP
* USA 2000 Fat Wreck Chords, LPSWINGSWIN LP
  Notes: San Francisco punk outfit includes their cover of "Eddie's Teddy", lyric sheet included.

THE BEST OF ROCKY RADIO
* USA 4711-1 Release: Issue #1
  Notes: The Best of Rocky Radio, Nathan Summers, Jim "Cosmo" Hetzer, Kev J. Boycik, and Reg Gables.

THE TIME WARP (EXTENDED VERSION)
* UK 1986 Howfree Limited/ Nidges Record Productions, 061-834-3403 test pressing acetate 12" PS
  The Time Warp (Extended Version) 45rpm, stereo
  Notes: scarce single-sided Test pressing featuring unique sleeve artwork which credits Damian as "Dame Damian". Later released by Sedition Records (EDITL 3311).

- UK 1987 Sedition Records, EDIT 3311 7" PS
  The Time Warp (Extended Version) / The Time Warp (7" Version), 45rpm, stereo,
  Notes: color sleeve artwork on yellow background containing head and shoulders photo of Damian with spiky yellow tipped hair.

- UK 1987 Sedition Records, EDITL 3311DJ promotional 12" PS
  The Time Warp (Extended Version) / The Time Warp (7" Version), Dancin', 45rpm, stereo
  Notes: color sleeve artwork on yellow background containing head and shoulders photo of Damian with spiky yellow tipped hair. Inner record label states "©1986 Howfree Limited".

- UK 1987 Sedition Records, EDITL 3311 12" PS
  The Time Warp (Extended Version) / The Time Warp (7" Version), Dancin', 45rpm, stereo
  Notes: color sleeve artwork on yellow background containing head and shoulders photo of Damian with spiky yellow tipped hair. Inner record label states "©1986 Howfree Limited".

- UK 1987 Sedition Records, EDITLX 3311 12" plain sleeve
  The Time Warp (Hands On Your Hips Mix) / The Time Warp (7" Version), 45rpm, stereo,
  Notes: Limited Edition release mixed by Pascal Gabriel and the only release to include this version.

THE TIME WARP II (BRAND NEW VERSION)
- UK 1987 Zomba Productions / Jive Records, JIVE 160 7" PS
  The Time Warp II (Brand New Version) (4:25) / Fight For What You Believe (4:20) 45rpm, stereo
  Notes: color sleeve artwork featuring Damian in leather jacket and chains. Cover states "The Dance from the Rocky Horror Show".

- UK 1987 Zomba Productions / Jive Records, test pressing 12", generic "Jive" sleeve
  The Time Warp II (Brand New Extended Version) (6:18) / The Time Warp (Original Version) (5:55)
  Fight For What You Believe (3:19), 45rpm, stereo,
  Notes: hand written details on plain white label, no catalogue number. Release date given as 7-12-87.

- HOLLAND 1987 Zomba Productions / Jive Records, JIVE:145378, 7" generic sleeve
  The Time Warp II (Brand New Version) (4:25) / Fight For What You Believe (4:20) 45rpm, stereo

- SOUTH AFRICA 1987 Jive Records, JIVS154, 7" PS
  The Time Warp II (Brand New Version) (4:25) / Fight For What You Believe (4:20) 45rpm, stereo,
  Notes: color sleeve artwork featuring Damian in leather jacket and chains. Cover states "The Dance from the Rocky Horror Show".

- UK 1988 Zomba Productions / Jive Records, JIVE R 160 12" PS
  The Time Warp II (Brand New Extended Version) (6:18) /The Time Warp II (Original Version) (4:25)
  Fight For What You Believe (3:19), 45rpm, stereo,
  Notes: new sleeve artwork features extreme close up of a grey clock with "Damian" and "Timewarp" in a red and white wavy font.

- UK 1987 Zomba Productions / Jive Records, JIVE R 160 12" PS
  The Time Warp II (Brand New Extended Version) (6:18) / The Time Warp (Original Version) (5:55)
  Fight For What You Believe (3:19), 45rpm, stereo,
  Notes: color sleeve artwork featuring Damian in leather jacket and chains. Cover states "The Dance from the Rocky Horror Show".

- HOLLAND 1987 Zomba Productions Limited, 6.20867 12" PS
  The Time Warp II (Brand New Extended Version) (6:18) / The Time Warp (Original Version) (5:55)
  Fight For What You Believe (3:19) 45rpm, stereo,
  Notes: color sleeve artwork featuring Damian in leather jacket and chains. Cover states "The Dance From The Rocky Horror Show"

- UK 1988 Zomba Productions / Jive Records, JIVE 160 7" PS
  The Time Warp II (Brand New Version) (4:25) / Fight For What You Believe (4:20) 45rpm, stereo
  Notes: new sleeve artwork features extreme close up of a grey clock with "Damian" and "Timewarp" in a red and white wavy font.

- GERMANY 1987 Jive Records, JIVE ZT5527 7" PS
  The Time Warp II (Brand New Extended Version) (6:18) / The Time Warp II (Original Version) (4:25)
  Fight For What You Believe (3:19), 45rpm, stereo,
  Notes: new sleeve artwork features extreme close up of a grey clock with "Damian" and "Timewarp" in a red and white wavy font.

- UK 1988 Zomba Productions / Jive Records, JIVE 182 7" PS
  The Time Warp II (Brand New Version) (4:25) / Fight For What You Believe (4:20) 45rpm, stereo
  Notes: new sleeve artwork features extreme close up of a grey clock with "Damian" and "Timewarp" in a red and white wavy font.

- UK 1988 Zomba Productions / Jive Records, JIVE T 182 12" PS
  The Time Warp II (Brand New Extended Version) (6:18) / The Time Warp II (Original Version) (4:25)
  Fight For What You believe (4:20) 45rpm, stereo
  Notes: new sleeve artwork features extreme close up of a grey clock with "Damian" and "Timewarp" in a red and white wavy font.

- UK 1988 Zomba Productions / Liberation Records, LMD 598 promotional 12" PS
  The Time Warp II (Brand New Extended Version) (6:18) / The Time Warp II (Original Version) (4:25)
  Fight For What You believe (4:20) 45rpm, stereo
  Notes: new sleeve artwork features extreme close up of a grey clock with "Damian" and "Timewarp" in a red and white wavy font.

THE TIME WARP (PWL REMIX)

- UK 1989 Zomba Productions /Jive Records, JIVE 209 7" PS
  The Time Warp (PWL Remix) (4:03) / Fight For What You Believe (4:20)
  Notes: different sleeve artwork features close up drawing of a grey wrist watch. "Damian" and "Time Warp" printed inside the watch face.

- AUSTRALIA 1989 Zomba Productions /BMG Records, JIVE 209 7" PS
  The Time Warp (PWL Remix) (4:03) / Fight For What You Believe (4:20) 45rpm, stereo
  Notes: different sleeve artwork features close up drawing of a grey wrist watch. "Damian" and "Time Warp" printed inside the watch face.

- SPAIN 1989 Jive Records, ZB-43213-1A 7" PS
  The Time Warp (PWL Remix) (4:03) / Fight For What You Believe (4:20) 45rpm, stereo
  Notes: different sleeve artwork features close up drawing of a grey wrist watch. "Damian" and "Time Warp" printed inside the watch face.

- GERMANY 1989 Jive Records, JIVE ZT43213 7" PS
  The Time Warp (PWL Remix) (4:03) / Fight For What You Believe (4:20) 45rpm, stereo
  Notes: different sleeve artwork features close up drawing of a grey wrist watch. "Damian" and "Time Warp" printed inside the watch face.

- GERMANY 1989 Jive Records, JIVE ZT43214 12" PS
  The Time Warp (PWL Extended Remix) (7:43) / The Time Warp (Original Version) (4:35)
  Fight For What You Believe (4:20) 45rpm, stereo
  Notes: different sleeve artwork features close up drawing of a grey wrist watch. "Damian" and "Time Warp" printed inside the watch face.

- UK 1989 Zomba Productions /Jive Records, PROMO 22 promotional 12" PS
  The Time Warp (PWL Extended Remix) (7:43), The Time Warp (7" Version) (4:03), The Time Warp (Original Version) (4:35)
  b/w The Time Warp II (Brand New Extended Version) (6:18), Fight For What You Believe (3:18) 45rpm, stereo
  Notes: released in generic sleeve containing large color "Damian" promo sticker on front sleeve.

- UK 1989 Zomba Productions /Jive Records, JIVE T 209 12" PS
  The Time Warp (PWL Extended Remix) (7:43), The Time Warp (7" Version) (4:03), The Time Warp (Original Version) (4:35)
  b/w The Time Warp II (Brand New Extended Version) (6:18), Fight For What You Believe (3:18) 45rpm, stereo
  Notes: different sleeve artwork features close up drawing of a grey wrist watch. "Damian" and "Time Warp" printed inside the watch face. This 12" features 4 different versions of The Time Warp!

- USA 1990 Zomba Ltd /BMG Records, 1426-1-JD 12" PS
  The Time Warp (PWL Extended Remix) (7:43), The Time Warp (7" Version) (4:03), The Time Warp (Original Version) (4:35)
  b/w The Time Warp II (Brand New Extended Version) (6:18), Fight For What You Believe (3:18) 45rpm, stereo
  Notes: different sleeve artwork features close up drawing of a grey wrist watch. "Damian" and "Time Warp" printed inside the watch face. This 12" features 4 different versions of The Time Warp!

WIG WAM BAM
- UK 1989 Zomba Ltd /BMG Records, JIVE 236 12" PS
  Wig Wam Bam / The Time Warp (PWL Remix) (4:03) 45rpm, stereo
  Notes: Damian's follow up single which included his Time Warp cover on side 2.

THE TIME WARP (NEW NINETIES VERSION)
- SCOTLAND 1998 Academy Street Records, ACSTO35 promotional 12", plain black sleeve
  The Time Warp (Extended Vocal Mix) (6:02) / The Time Warp (Over 18's Under Sedation Mix) (5:49),
  Molecular Breakdown (3:38) 45rpm, stereo
  Notes: Damian's all new version of the track recorded almost a decade later!

- SCOTLAND 1998 Academy Street Records, ACSTO35 12", generic "Academy Street" sleeve
  The Time Warp (Extended Vocal Mix) (6:02) / The Time Warp (Over 18's Under Sedation Mix) (5:49)
  Molecular Breakdown (3:38) 45rpm, stereo
  Notes: Damian's all new version of the track recorded almost a decade later!

RICHARD O'BRIEN RELATED

TRUTH & BEAUTY (Featuring Little Nell as Roxanne)
- UK 1974 Rak Records, RAK 181 demonstration 7", generic "Rak Records" sleeve, Tuff Little Surfer Boy / Touch-A Touch-A Touch Me 45rpm

Notes: Label states "Demo Record Not For Sale". Track one written by "Kramer", track 2 by (O'Brien) from "The Rocky Horror Show". Produced by Andrew O'Bonzo for Rich Teaboy Productions/Druidcrest Music. Release date listed as "2-8-74". Vinyl groove etching: side A: "BLAIR", side B: "NAUGHTY".

HANG 11 (MUTANT SURF PUNKS) – VARIOUS ARTISTS

* UK 1985 Anagram Records, GRAM 23 LP
  Notes: Various Artists compilation featuring Tuff Little Surfer Boy by Truth & Beauty on Side 2.

* GREECE 1985 Cherry Red/Music-Box, B RED 63 LP
  Notes: Various Artists compilation featuring Tuff Little Surfer Boy by Truth & Beauty on Side 2.

DICKY HART & THE PALPITATIONS - THAT'S A NO NO (KNEES VERBOTEN)

* UK 1975 Philips / Phonogram Records, 6006 455 7", generic "Philips Records" sleeve
  That's A No No (Knees Verboten) / Master Of My Machine 45rpm, mono
  Notes: track one written by R. O'Brien / J. Sinclair, track 2 by "C LaZero". Produced by Andrew O'Bonzo for Rich Teaboy Productions. Both sides recorded in MONO. Richard O'Brien sings "That's A No No (Knees Verboten)" [NB: In 1984 a different group also called Dicky Hart & The Palpitations released a single titled "Hungry For You" on Medical Records however this is in no way connected with Ritz O'Brien!].

ROLLOX

* UK 1975 Pye Records, 7N 45494 7", generic "Pye Records" sleeve, Funky Sailor / You Know What Amin 45rpm, mono
  Notes: track one written by "Trad, arranged by Rollox", track 2 by "Blair, Kenzie, Hill, Cowan, Rowley". Produced by Andrew O'Bonzo for Rich Teaboy Productions / Druidcrest Music. Both sides recorded in MONO. Side 1 is an instrumental track.

THE STRIPPER - THE SYDNEY THEATRE COMPANY

* AUSTRALIA 1982 RCA Limited, VPL1 LP, gatefold jacket
  Notes: Lyrics by Richard O'Brien, music by Richard Hartley. Produced by Spencer Lee, Peter Plavsic, & Michael Tyack for The Sydney Theatre Company. This was the Original Cast recording from the musical staged at the Kinselas Theatre, Sydney. Directed & designed by Brian Thomson.

KIMI & RITZ

MERRY CHRISTMAS BABY

- UK 1973 CBS/Epic Records, S EPC 1971 demonstration 7", generic Epic sleeve
  Merry Christmas Baby (3:50) / Eddie (3:48) 45rpm, stereo, mono
  Notes: "Promotion Copy Not For Sale", Large red promo"A" printed across label, side 1 is recorded in stereo and side 2 in MONO, tracks written by "R. O'Brien" & music arranged by Robin Sylvester. B-side just credits KIMI as the artist for "Eddie" and label text reads: "Eddie (R. O'Brien)(From the Rocky Horror Show)", "Release Date 7th Dec, 1973". This is a slightly shorter remixed version of the original release.

- UK 1973 CBS/Epic Records, EPC 1971 7", generic Epic sleeve
  Merry Christmas Baby (4:55) / Eddie (3:48), 45rpm, mono
  Notes: This is the standard commercial release with both sides recorded in MONO, tracks written by "R. O'Brien" & music arranged by Robin Sylvester. B-side just credits KIMI as the artist for "Eddie" and label reads: "Eddie (R. O'Brien)(From the Rocky Horror Show)". This is the only release to include the complete & unedited original version.

- UK 1974 CBS/Epic Records, EPC 1971 7", generic Epic sleeve
  Merry Christmas Baby (DJ Version) (3:59) / Eddie (3:48) 45rpm, stereo, mono
  Notes: side 1 recorded in stereo and side 2 in MONO, tracks written by "R. O'Brien" & music arranged by Robin Sylvester. B-side just credits KIMI as the artist for "Eddie". "Release Date 22nd Nov, 1974" This was a 1974 reissue of the same remixed version from the 1973 DJ promo release.

I WAS IN LOVE WITH DANNY BUT THE CROWD WAS IN LOVE WITH DEAN

- UK 1975 CBS/Epic Records, S EPC 3018 demonstration 7", generic Epic sleeve
  I Was In Love With Danny But The Crowd Was In Love With Dean (3:03) / Pseud's Corner (2:40) 45rpm, stereo
  Notes: "Promotion Copy Not For Sale", Large red "A" printed across label, tracks written by "R. O'Brien", music arranged by Richard Hartley and produced by Andrew O'Bonzo for Rich Teaboy Productions/ Druidcrest Music. B-side just credits RITZ as the artist for Pseud's Corner. Release date listed as "21st Feb 1975", the demo pressing misspells Richard Hartley as "Hareley".

- UK 1975 CBS/Epic Records, S EPC 3018 7", generic Epic sleeve
  I Was In Love With Danny But The Crowd Was In Love With Dean (3:03) / Pseud's Corner (2:40) 45rpm, stereo
  Notes: Tracks written by "R. O'Brien", music arranged by Richard Hartley and produced by Andrew O'Bonzo for Rich Teaboy Productions/Druidcrest Music. B-side only credits RITZ as the artist for Pseud's Corner.

BARRY BOSTWICK

THE KLOWNS – LADY LOVE
* USA 1970 RCA/Victor Records, 0393 7" PS
  Lady Love (3:34) / *If* You Can't Be A Clown (2:47) 45rpm, stereo
  Notes: single taken from The Klowns' soundtrack "Ringling Bros & Barnum & Bailey". 'Lady Love' performed by Barry Bostwick.

THE KLOWNS - RINGLING BROS & BARNUM & BAILEY
* USA 1970 RCA/Victor Records, LSP-4438 gatefold LP
  Notes: Barry Bostwick was one of The Klowns' lead singers.

GREASE – ORIGINAL BROADWAY CAST ALBUM
* USA 1972 MGM Records, SE34 LP
  Notes: Barry Bostwick originated the role of Danny Zuko and sings on several tracks.

* CANADA 1972 RCA MUSIC CLUB, R133606 LP
  Notes: Barry Bostwick originated the role of Danny Zuko and sings on several tracks.

* AUSTRALIA 1978 MGM Records / Polydor Australia, 2315 111 LP
  Notes: 1978 Australian release. Back cover includes photos from the production.

THE ROBBER BRIDEGROOM – ORIGINAL BROADWAY CAST ALBUM
* USA 1976 Columbia Records, P14589 LP
  Notes: Original Broadway Cast recording of The Robber Bridegroom starring Barry Bostwick, composed by Robert Waldman.

LITTLE NELL

STILETTOS AND LIPSTICK
* UK 1975 A&M Records Ltd, AMS 7194 7", generic A&M Sleeve
  Stilettos And Lipstick (2:19) / Do the Swim (Splash Splash) (2:23) 45rpm, stereo
  Notes: Both tracks are different to the standard versions. Released on 08 September, 1975. Vinyl groove etching: side A: "A Porky Prime Cut" side B: "Do The Pork Oink Oink".

BEAUTY QUEEN/BEAUTY QUEEN (SLOW VERSION)
*   Australia 1980 Charisma Records 6000 648 7"Single Generic Sleeve
    Notes: On stock Charisma label with mad hatter image.

SEE YOU ROUND LIKE A RECORD
*   UK 1976 A&M Records Ltd, AMS 7221 7", generic A&M Sleeve
    See You Round Like A Record (2:44) / Dance That Cocktail Latin Way (3:34) 45rpm, stereo

*   AUSTRALIA 1976 Festival Records, K-6388 7", generic Festival Sleeve
    See You Round Like A Record (2:45) / Dance That Cocktail Latin Way (3:07) 45rpm, stereo *Notes: no US release.*
    "See You Round Like A Record" was included as the b-side of "Fever" 2 years later.

FEVER (ORIGINAL 1976 RELEASE)
*   UK 1976 A & M Records Ltd, AMS 7234 7", generic A&M Sleeve
    Fever (2:36) / Do The Swim (2:30) 45rpm, stereo
    *Notes: "Fever" on this recording is different to all other versions of the track. Very few copies pressed --
    EXTREMELY RARE!! This original version was shelved, re-mixed, and officially released 2 years later in 1978.
    The flip side features the standard single version of "Do the Swim (Splash Splash) previously released as the
    b-side on Stilettos And Lipstick. Vinyl groove etching: side A: "ARUN" side B: (no wording).*

*   UK 1978 A&M Records Ltd, AMS 7374-DJ promotional 7" PS
    Fever (3:11) / See You Round Like A Record (2:46) 45 rpm, stereo
    *Notes: A&M label art is standard brown and grey with promo stamp printed in the center. This promotional release contains
    another mix of Fever exclusive only to this pressing! Different to the 1976.*

*   UK 1978 A&M Records Ltd, AMS 7374 promotional 7" PS
    Fever (3:11) / See You Round Like A Record (2:46) 45 rpm, stereo
    *Notes: A&M label art is yellow and orange with promo stamp printed in the center. This promotional release contains another
    mix of Fever exclusive only to this pressing! Different to the 1976 release (and all yellow vinyl pressings of the single even
    though it has the same catalogue number as the standard yellow vinyl release). "See You Round Like A Record" is the standard
    mix as all other releases.*

*   UK 1978 A&M Records Ltd, AMS 7374-DJ promotional 7" PS
    Fever (3:11) / See You Round Like A Record (2:46) 45 rpm, stereo
    Notes: A&M label art is standard brown and grey with promo stamp printed in the centre.

THE MUSICAL WORLD OF LITTLE NELL -- AQUATIC TEENAGE SEX & SQUALOR (1978)
*   UK 1975 A&M Records Ltd, AMS 7351 7" promotional red vinyl PS
    Do The Swim (2:30) / 1. Stilettos and Lipstick (2:37) 2. Dance That Cocktail Latin Way (Tropical Isle) (3:09) 45rpm, stereo
    Notes: promo stamp printed on label.

*   UK 1975 A&M Records Ltd, AMS 7351 red vinyl PS 7"
    Do The Swim (2:30) / 1.Stilettos And Lipstick (2:37) 2. Dance That Cocktail Latin Way (Tropical Isle) (3:09) 45rpm, stereo
    *Notes: This is the repackaged 1978 re-issue of the original "Do The Swim" 7" single. It includes images on the back
    cover of films which Nell appeared in from 1975 -- 1977. The back sleeve also (strangely) claims this to be "The first triple
    b-side record in recording history" which is probably referring to the fact that all tracks were originally released as b-side
    songs. In all of the above pressings, the word "stilettos" is misspelt "stillettos" on the inner record label*

*   UK 1975 A&M Records Ltd, AMS 7351 7" PS
    Do The Swim (2:30) / 1.Stilettos And Lipstick (2:37) 2. Dance That Cocktail Latin Way (Tropical Isle) (3:09) 45rpm, stereo
    Notes: re-issue on standard black vinyl.

*   7o Aniversario Exito 1090
    Venezuela 1978 A&M Records LPS-88653
    *Notes: compilation album that features Little Nell's "See You Round Like A Record", titled in Spanish as "Eres Redonda
    Como Un Disco"*

- AUSTRALIA 1975 Festival Records, K-7154 red vinyl 7" PS
  Do The Swim (2:30) / 1.Stilettos And Lipstick (2:37) 2. Dance That Cocktail Latin Way (Tropical Isle) (3:09) 45rpm, stereo

- PORTUGAL 1975 A&M Records Ltd, PAMS 7351 7" PS
  Do The Swim (2:30) / 1.Stilettos And Lipstick (2:37) 2. Dance That Cocktail Latin Way (Tropical Isle) (3:09) 45rpm, stereo
  Notes: back of sleeve is plain white, no images.

DO THE SWIM
- AUSTRALIA 1975 Festival Records, K-7154 7", generic Festival sleeve
  Do The Swim (2:37) / 1. Stilettos And Lipstick (2:25) 2. Tropical Isle (3:01) 45rpm, stereo
  Notes: "stilettos" is misspelt "stillettos". "Dance That Cocktail Latin Way was re-named as Tropical Isle.

FEVER (1978 RELEASE)
- UK 1978 A&M Records Ltd, AMS 7374 promotional 7" PS
  Fever (3:11) / See You Round Like A Record (2:46) 45 rpm, stereo
  Notes: A&M label art is yellow and orange with promo stamp printed in the center. This promotional release contains another mix of Fever exclusive only to this pressing! Different to the 1976 release (and all yellow vinyl pressings of the single even though it has the same catalogue number as the standard yellow vinyl release). "See You Round Like A Record" is the standard mix as all other releases.

- UK 1978 A&M Records Ltd, AMS 7374-DJ promotional 7" PS
  Fever (3:11) / See You Round Like A Record (2:46) 45 rpm, stereo
  Notes: A&M label art is standard brown and grey with promo stamp printed in the center.

- USA 1978 A&M Records Inc, AMS 2183 promotional 7", generic A&M Sleeve
  Fever (3:11) stereo / Fever (3:11) mono. 45rpm, stereo
  Notes: cut out jukebox hole

- USA 1978 A&M Records Inc, AMS 2183 promotional 7", generic A&M Sleeve
  Fever (3:11) / See You Round Like A Record (2:46) 45rpm, stereo
  Notes: cut out jukebox hole

- UK 1978 A&M Records Ltd, AMS 7374 BRIGHT yellow vinyl 7" PS
  Fever (3:11) / See You Round Like A Record (2:46) 45rpm, stereo

- UK 1978 A&M Records Ltd, AMS 7374 CLEAR yellow (transparent) vinyl 7" PS
  Fever (3:11) / See You Round Like A Record (2:46) 45rpm, stereo
  Notes: the yellow vinyl 7" had two separate pressings on remarkably different shades of yellow wax. The CLEAR yellow (see thru) vinyl is completely transparent and much rarer than the regular (bright) yellow pressing.

- SOUTH AFRICA 1978 A&M Records Ltd, AMRS 1254 7" PS, generic A&M Sleeve
  Fever (3:11) / See You Round Like A Record (2:46) 45rpm, stereo

FEVER (PROMOTIONAL FAN KIT)
- UK 1978 A&M Records Ltd, AMSP 7374 PROMOTIONAL FEVER FAN KIT: 7" on CLEAR yellow (transparent) vinyl PS
  Fever - Extended Version (5:06) / See You Round Like A Record (2:46) 45rpm, stereo
  Notes: packaged in a leopard print box with Nell button badge & Fever flick book! The inner record label on the 7" in this promo fan kit, has the incorrect information; It claims the track is the standard single version but it actually contains the extended 12" version! This particular yellow vinyl is different yet again to both other pressings -featuring a light greenish tint. Vinyl groove etching: side A: "Edited Version" side B: (no wording). No Australian release.

- UK 1978 A&M Records Ltd, AMSP 7374 PROMOTIONAL FEVER FAN KIT: 7" on CLEAR yellow (transparent) vinyl PS
  Fever - Extended Version (5:06) / See You Round Like A Record (2:46) 45rpm, stereo

FEVER (EXTENDED 12")
- UK 1978 A&M Records Ltd, AMSP 7374 promotional 12", generic "A&M Disco" sleeve
  Fever (5:06) / See You Round Like A Record (2:46) 45rpm, stereo
  Notes: this UK promo 12" oddly has the same catalogue number as the promotional Fever Fan Kit (AMSP 7374)

- USA 1978 A&M Records Inc, SP-12031 promotional 12", generic "A&M Disco" sleeve
Fever (Long Version) (5:06) / Fever (Short Version) (3:11) 33 1/3 rpm, stereo
Notes: sticker on cover reads "LITTLE NELL performing the disco version of the classic – FEVER"

- USA 1978 A&M Records Inc, SP-12031 promotional 12", generic "A&M Disco" sleeve
Fever (5:06) / See You Round Like A Record (2:46) 33 1/3 rpm, stereo

BEAUTY QUEEN (ORIGINAL MOTION PICTURE SCORE)
- UK 1980 Charisma Records, PRE 004 7" PS
Beauty Queen (2:30) / Slow Version (2:44) 45rpm, stereo
Notes: Nell performed this track as the opening number in the film "I Wanna Be A Beauty Queen" also known as "The Alternative Miss World". Vinyl groove etching: side A: "A GREAT FILM ANDREW" side B: "BUY SOME FOR LULU".
AUSTRALIA 1980 PolyGram Records, MX198287 (6000 648) 7", generic PolyGram sleeve, Beauty Queen (2:30) /
Slow Version (2:30) 45rpm, stereo *Notes: Vinyl etchings not repeated on Australian issue. No US release.*

LONDON HEAT WAVE (*VARIOUS ARTISTS*)
- JAPAN 1980 ALFA Records Inc /A&M Records, AMP-28008 LP, gatefold cover
Notes: A&M Records various Artists compilation released exclusively for Japanese promotion. Featuring the following 2 tracks by Little Nell; Side 1, track 2: Fever (3:14) & side 2, track 2: See You Round Like A Record (2:46). Includes insert sheets.

TIM CURRY

BABY LOVE
- USA 1976 Ode Records, ODE 66117 promotional 7", generic A&M sleeve
Baby Love (stereo) (3:42) / Baby Love (mono) (3:42) 45rpm
Notes: label states "Promotion Copy Not For Sale" Jukebox cut-out hole

- USA 1976 Ode Records, ODE 66117-S 7", generic A&M sleeve
Baby Love (3:42) / Just Fourteen (3:55) 45rpm, stereo
Notes: Brian Wilson from The Beach Boys (and wife Marilyn Rovell Wilson) both sing backing vocals on "Just Fourteen" Jukebox cut-out hole.

- UK 1976 A&M / Ode Records, ODS 66117 7", generic paper sleeve
Baby Love (3:42) / Just Fourteen (3:55) 45rpm, stereo

WE WENT AS FAR AS WE FELT LIKE GOIN'

* USA 1976 Ode Records, ODE-66113-S promotional 10", generic A&M sleeve
Went As Far As We Felt Like Goin' (stereo) / Went As Far As We Felt Like Goin' (mono) 45rpm
Notes: label states "Promotion Copy Not For Sale". Both these tracks(together with Baby Love & Just Fourteen), were outtakes from an unreleased Tim Curry album recorded in 1976 and produced by Lou Adler.

WE WENT AS FAR AS WE FELT LIKE GOIN'

* USA 1976 Ode Records, promotional 12", generic A&M sleeve
We Went As Far As We Felt Like Going / Biting My Nails 45rpm, stereo
Notes: label states "Promotion Copy Not For Sale". Both these tracks(together with Baby Love & Just Fourteen), were outtakes from an unreleased Tim Curry album recorded in 1976 and produced by Lou Adler.

I WILL

* USA 1978 A&M Records, 2105 promotional 7", generic A&M sleeve
I Will (stereo) (3:44) / I Will (mono) (3:44) 45rpm, stereo

* UK 1978 A&M Records, AMS7383 promotional 7" PS
I Will (3:44) / Brontosaurus (4:38) 45rpm, stereo *Notes: cover art features black and white Tim photo with folded arms. Label states "Promotion Copy Not For Sale"*

* UK 1978 A&M Records, AMS7383 7" PS, I Will (3:44) / Brontosaurus (4:38) 45rpm, stereo
Notes: cover art features black and white Tim photo with folded arms

* HOLLAND 1978 A&M Records, AMS6632 7" PS, I Will (3:41) / Brontosaurus (4:38) 45rpm, stereo
Notes: cover art features color close-up of Tim's face with messy hair on a yellow background. Jukebox cut-out hole.

* AUSTRALIA 1978 Festival Records, K7291 7", generic "Festival Records" sleeve
I Will (3:45) / Brontosaurus (4:36) 45rpm, stereo

* NEW ZEALAND 1978 Festival Records (NZ) Ltd, K7291 7", generic "Festival Records (NZ)" sleeve
I Will (3:45) / Brontosaurus (4:36) 45rpm, stereo

BIRDS OF A FEATHER

* USA 1978 A&M Records, 2079 promotional 7", generic A&M sleeve
Birds Of A Feather (stereo) (3:35) / Birds Of A Feather (mono) (3:35) 45rpm

* CANADA 1978 A&M Records, 2079 promotional 7", generic A&M sleeve
Birds Of A Feather (stereo) (3:35) / Birds Of A Feather (mono) (3:35) 45rpm
Notes: large red "A"(promo mark) printed over centre label, Jukebox cut-out hole.

* USA 1978 A&M Records, 2079 7", generic A&M sleeve
Birds Of A Feather / Brontosaurus 45rpm, stereo

* UK 1978 A&M Records, AMS 7411 demonstrational 7" PS
Birds Of A Feather / Brontosaurus 45rpm, stereo

* CANADA 1978 A&M Records, 12524 7", generic A&M sleeve
Birds Of A Feather / Brontosaurus 45rpm, stereo

* GERMANY 1978 A&M Records, AMS6853 promotional white label 7" PS
Birds Of A Feather / Brontosaurus 45rpm, stereo
Notes: cover features black and white pic of Tim from the inner sleeve of "Read My Lips". Back cover is orange with promo info written in German.

* GERMANY 1978 A&M Records, AMS6853 7" PS
Birds Of A Feather / Brontosaurus 45rpm, stereo
Notes: cover features black and white pic of Tim from the inner sleeve of "Read My Lips".

I DO THE ROCK

* USA 1979 A&M Records, 2166-S promotional white label 7" PS
I Do The Rock (Long Version) (4:45) / I Do The Rock (Edited Version) (3:02) 45rpm, stereo.
Notes: sleeve art features printed song lyrics, front cover states "Promotion Copy Not For Sale" Jukebox cut-out hole.

* USA 1979 A&M Records, 2166-S 7", generic A&M sleeve
I Do The Rock (Long Version) (4:45) / I Do The Rock (Edited Version) (3:02) 45rpm, stereo.

* UK 1979 A&M Records, AMS 7470 demonstrational 7" PS
I Do The Rock (3:02) / Hide This Face (2:54) 45rpm, stereo
Notes: released with silver picture sleeve showing Tim's face, also includes lyrics to "I Do The Rock" printed on back. Label states "Promotion Copy Not For Sale".

* UK 1979 A&M Records, AMS 7470 7" PS
I Do The Rock (3:02) / Hide This Face (2:54) 45rpm, stereo
Notes: released with silver picture sleeve showing Tim's face, also includes lyrics to "I Do The Rock" printed on back.

* AUSTRALIA 1979 Festival Records, K-7635 7", generic "Festival Records" sleeve
I Do The Rock (4:45) / Hide This Face (2:54) 45rpm, stereo

* GERMANY 1979 A&M Records, AMS 7630 7" PS
I Do The Rock (4:45) / Hide This Face (2:54) 45rpm, stereo
Notes: released with silver picture sleeve showing Tim's face, also includes lyrics to "I Do The Rock" printed on back Jukebox cut-out hole

* CANADA 1979 A&M Records, AM2166 7" PS, generic A&M sleeve
I Do The Rock (Long Version) (4:45) / Hide This Face (2:54) 45rpm, stereo
Notes: Jukebox cut-out hole

* USA 1996 A&M Records, 75021-8570-7 split juke-box promotional 7", generic sleeve
I Do The Rock / Another Lover by Giant Steps, 45rpm, stereo
Notes: Tim track features on one side only

* USA 1979 A&M Records, SP-17093, promotional 12" PS
I Do The Rock / Paradise Garage (edit) & Charge It (edit) 33 1/3 rpm, stereo
Notes: picture sleeve art features printed song lyrics

* USA 1979 A&M Records, SP-17103 promotional 12" PS, generic A&M sleeve
I Do The Rock (4:45) / Paradise Garage (6:12) 33 1/3 rpm, stereo

PARADISE GARAGE

* GERMANY 1980 A&M Records, AMS 7655 7" PS
Paradise Garage (4:01) / Charge It (4:00) 45rpm, stereo
Notes: color picture sleeve featuring 7 composite photos of Tim's face. German only issue Jukebox cut-out hole

* GERMANY 1980 A&M Records, AMS 12.7655 12" PS
Paradise Garage (6:12) / Charge It (5:16) 45rpm, stereo
Notes: color picture sleeve featuring 7 composite photos of Tim's face. German only issue. Also includes an A&M Records, German press release sheet from April 1980 for Paradise Garage (text written in German).

WORKING ON MY TAN

* USA 1981 A&M Records, 2353 promotional 7", generic A&M sleeve
Working On My Tan (stereo) (3:48) / Working On My Tan (mono) (3:48) 45rpm
Notes: Jukebox cut-out hole

* USA 1981 A&M Records, 2353-S 7" PS, Working On My Tan (3:48) / On A Roll (2:49) 45rpm, stereo
Notes: color picture sleeve featuring Tim in swimming pool. Jukebox cut-out hole

- AUSTRALIA 1981 Festival Records, K-8376 7", generic "Festival Records" sleeve
  Working On My Tan (Edited Version) (3:48) / On A Roll (2:49) 45rpm, stereo

- SOUTH AFRICA 1981 A&M Records, AMRS 1366 7", generic A&M sleeve
  Working On My Tan (3:48) / On A Roll (2:49) 45rpm, stereo

- HOLLAND 1981 A&M Records, AMS-9143 7" PS
  Working On My Tan (4:06) / On A Roll (2:49) 45rpm, stereo
  Notes: color picture sleeve featuring Tim in swimming pool. Jukebox cut-out hole

- SPAIN 1981 CBS / A&M Records, AMS 9143 PS 7"
  Bronceandome (Working on my Tan) (4:06) / On A Roll (2:49) 45rpm, stereo
  Notes: Spanish issue contains different sleeve art - featuring photo of Tim from the Simplicity insert sleeve, Song lyrics printed in English on back cover

WORKING ON MY TAN
- USA 1981 Masterdisk/A&M Records, promotional DJ acetate 12"
  Working On My Tan (Club Mix) (6:08) 33 1/3 rpm, stereo
  Notes: single-sided, extremely thick, acetate vinyl (side 2 is blank) Contains no catalogue number, re-mixed on 16 June, 1981 at Masterdisk Corporation, New York City. This mix is a previously unreleased version.

SIMPLICITY
- USA 1981 A&M Records, 2376 promotional 7", generic A&M sleeve
  Simplicity (stereo) (3:59) / Simplicity (mono) (3:59) 45rpm
  Notes: Label states "Promotion Copy Not For Sale" Jukebox cut-out hole.

- USA 1981 A&M Records, 2376-S 7", generic A&M sleeve
  Simplicity (3:59) / Betty Jean (3:20) 45rpm, stereo

- USA 1981 A&M Records, AM 2376, 7" PS
  Simplicity (3:59) / Betty Jean (3:20) 45rpm, stereo

- HOLLAND 1981 A&M Records, AMS 9180 7" PS
  Simplicity (3:59) / Betty Jean (3:20) 45rpm, stereo
  Notes: black & white cover art featuring head and shoulders photo of Tim in brown jacket with collar turned up, Jukebox cut-out hole.

- GERMANY 1981 A&M Records, AMS 9180 7" PS
  Simplicity (3:59) / Betty Jean (3:20) 45rpm, stereo
  Notes: black & white cover art featuring head and shoulders photo of Tim in brown jacket with collar turned up.

READ MY LIPS
- USA 1978 A&M Records, SP 4717 white label promotional LP
  Notes: includes original lyric sleeve & comes with promo tent card for display (double sided showing Tim images).

- USA 1978 A&M Records, SP 4717 white label promotional LP
  Notes: includes original lyric sleeve &includes cover sticker 'warning' that reads: "Dear Programmer: The songs "Sloe Gin" and "Alan" each contain one of the seven dirty words and are not suitable for airplay". Back cover bears a small "Promotional Record for Broadcast and Review NOT FOR SALE" sticker in the lower right corner.

- USA 1978 A&M Records, SP 4717 LP
  Notes: includes original photo sleeve insert.

- GERMANY 1978 A&M Records, AMLH64717 LP
  Notes: includes original photo sleeve insert.

- GERMANY 1978 A&M Records, AMLH64717 demonstrational LP
  Notes: includes original photo sleeve insert. Front cover features different layout of text &a gold sticker stating "Der Star der Rocky Horror Picture Show".

- AUSTRALIA 1978 Festival Records, L 36714 LP
  Notes: includes original photo sleeve insert

- CANADA 1978 A&M Records, SP 4717 promotional LP
  Notes: includes original photo sleeve insert

- CANADA 1978 A&M Records, SP 4717 LP
  Notes: includes original photo sleeve insert

- UK 1978 A&M Records, AM64717 LP
  Notes: includes original photo sleeve insert

- SOUTH AFRICA 1978 Interpak / A&M Records, AMLH 64717 LP
  Notes: cover printed on thicker,glossy cardboard, includes original photo sleeve insert.

- HOLLAND 1978 A&M Records, AM64717 LP
  Notes: includes original photo sleeve insert.

FEARLESS

- USA 1979 A&M Records, SP 4773 white label test pressing LP
  Notes: no album cover sleeves. States on inner record label: "Not yet approved (limited distribution)".
  Date pressed: 5-24-79.

- USA 1979 A&M Records, SP 4773 promotional LP
  Notes: gold promo stamp. Includes original lyric insert sleeve.

- USA 1979 A&M Records, SP 4773 LP
  Notes: includes original lyric sheet insert sleeve.

- *CANADA 1979 A&M Records, SP4773 LP*
  Notes: includes original lyric sheet insert sleeve.

- AUSTRALIA 1979 A&M / Festival Records, L 36947 promotional LP
  Notes: stamped promo issue containing press release bio sheets and 2 publicity photos. Also includes original lyric sheet insert sleeve.

- AUSTRALIA 1979 A&M / Festival Records, L 36947 LP
  Notes: includes original lyric sheet insert sleeve.

- NEW ZEALAND 1979 A&M /Festival Records, L 36947 LP
  Notes: includes original lyric sheet insert sleeve.

- GERMANY 1979 A&M Records, SP4773 (SP 5283) LP
  Notes: includes original lyric sheet insert sleeve.

- NORWAY 1979 A&M Records, CB271 LP
  Notes: includes original lyric sheet insert sleeve.

- HOLLAND 1979 A&M Records, AMLH64773 LP
  Notes :released in The Netherlands with completely unique cover artwork (similar to the graphics on "Paradise Garage" German 12" single).

- UK 1979 A&M Records, AMLH64773 LP
  Notes: includes original lyric sheet insert sleeve.

- SOUTH AFRICA 1979 Interpak / A&M Records, AMLH 64773 LP
  Notes: cover printed on thicker, glossy cardboard, includes lyric sheet insert sleeve.

- ITALY 1979 A&M Records, CB271 LP
  Notes: includes original lyric sheet insert sleeve.

SIMPLICITY

- USA 1981 A&M Records, SP4830 promotional LP
  Notes: gold promo stamp. Includes original photo sleeve insert & label bears standard A&M logo.

- USA 1981 A&M Records, SP4830 promotional white label LP
  Notes: gold promo stamp. Includes original photo sleeve insert &unique white label artwork featuring Tim photo from back of album jacket.

- USA 1981 A&M Records, SP4830 LP
  Notes: includes original photo sleeve insert.

- UK 1981 A&M Records, AMLH64830 LP
  Notes: includes original photo sleeve insert.

- AUSTRALIA 1981 Festival Records, L 37616 promotional LP
  Notes: promo sticker on inner label which bears standard A&M logo. Includes original photo sleeve insert.

- AUSTRALIA 1981 Festival Records, L 37616 LP
  Notes: includes original photo sleeve insert.

- CANADA 1981 A&M Records, SP4830 LP
  Notes: includes original photo sleeve insert.

- HOLLAND 1981 A&M Records, AMLH64830 LP
  Notes: includes original photo sleeve insert.

- GERMANY 1981 A&M Records, 639823 LP
  Notes: includes original photo sleeve insert.

COMPACT DISC'S

- The Rocky Horror Show, Germany 1994 No label or catalog number
  Notes: EP release of the Dreseden, Germany cast

- The Rocky Horror Show
  Argentina 1994 No label or cat number
  Notes: Del Globo Theatre, Buenos Aires. Sung in Spanish.

- The Rocky Horror Show
  Germany 1995 Private Release No label or cat number
  Notes: Recorded by the TIC (Theatre In Cronenberg) stage cast and initially only sold at the theatre. Sung in English.

- The Rocky Horror Show
  Finland 1995 Poplandia Music HORROR666
  Notes: Sung entirely in Finnish.

- The Rocky Horror Show
  Denmark 1996 Aarhus Theater/Rocky Horror Company Ltd. (Private Release No Cat Number)
  Notes: 3 song EP sold at the theatre. Language switches between English and Danish.

- The Rocky Horror Show
  Norway 1996 Chateau Neuf No Cat Number Promotional
  Notes: 4 song promo EP for the production at Chateau Neuf in Olso, Norway.

- The Rocky Horror Show: Silver Jubilee
  South Africa 1997 BMG Africa Records CDBSP (LF) 7016
  Notes: South African stage cast recording. Sung in English.

- The Rocky Horror Show
  Germany 1999 Audare / C.A.B. Records No Cat Number
  Notes: Recorded in Bamberg, Germany. Sung in English.

- The Rocky Horror Show
  Peru 2001 TIM Peru recordings no cat number
  Notes: Peruvian stage cast recording. Sung completely in Spanish.

- The Rocky Horror Show
  Germany 2008 BBP Records Private Release No Cat number Promotional
  Notes: 3 song EP sung in English.

- El Show De Terror De Rocky (The Rocky Horror Show)
  Mexico 2009 Magic Sound Records
  Notes: Stage cast recording. Sung completely in Spanish.

- The Rocky Horror Show
  Iceland 2010 Leikfélag Akureyrar No cat number
  Notes: Stage cast recording. Sung in Iclandic.

- The Rocky Horror Show
  Japan 2011 Parco Recodings PTCD-18
  Notes: Stage cast recording. Sung entirely in Japanese.

8 TRACKS:

THE ROCKY HORROR PICTURE SHOW ORIGINAL SOUNDTRACK
- USA 1979 OdeRecords (21653 N)/GRT Tapes 8374-21653 N)
  Notes: First release of the soundtrack distributed by GRT Tapes. Blue Cartridge.

- USA 1979 Ode Records/Jem Records OSV-8-21653
  Notes: Second release of the soundtrack in the US on 8 tack. First edition of this release comes in a brown slipcase and brown cartridge. Second edition comes in a black cartridge.

- Canada 1975 Ode Records ODEA-21653
  Notes: First edition comes in an orange cartridge. Second edition comes in a black cartridge.

THE ROCKY HORROR SHOW ORIGINAL ROXY CAST
- USA 1974 Ode/A&M Records 8T-77026
  Notes: First US 8 Track release comes in a black and white Ode Records slipcase and an olive green cartridge.

- USA 1979 Ode/Jem Records ODE-8-9009
  Notes: Second US Release
  Notes: Comes in a black cartridge.

- Original Australian Cast
  Australia 1974 Festival Records T35231
  Notes: In a white cartridge.

- Original London Cast
  Australia 1973 UK Records/EMI Records 8X SKLA 7706
  Notes: Australian release of them London Cast Recording. Comes in a white cartridge.

REEL TO REEL:

- The Rocky Horror Picture Show Original Soundtrack
  USA 1975 ODE/A&M no catalog number PROMOTIONAL
  Notes: Split into Two reels, side one on one reel and side 2 on the other reel. As we all know, the soundtrack was not released in the US until 1979, long after the A&M/Ode partnership had expired. So, this had to be some type of in office promo. Has the A&M records US address on it, so it's definitely of US origin.

THANK YOU'S

Without the aid and assistance from these people the updated Audience Participation Guide/Collector's Section would not have been possible. First, I would like to thank the original authors of the Audience Participation Guide: *Sal Piro and Mike Hess*

Much of information in this updated collector's guide was provided by:

Kev J. Boycik	*Mark Jabara Ellison*	*Bruce Cutter*
John Davey	*Tony Pazuzu*	

With support and assistance from the following individuals:

Chris Holley	*Rob Bagnall*	*Bill Brennan*
David Driskell	*James Norman*	*Gene Chiovari*
Ruth Fink-Winter	*Shon Cope*	*Shawn Hall*
Larry Viezel	*Richard Davidson Jr.*	*Shawn McHorse*
Brian Dempsey	*David Freeman*	*Steve VanMeter*
Mad Man Mike Ellenbogen		

And finally, thank you to my loving family. Thank you for being so supportive and patient while I worked on this book: *Dawn Marie, Page Maher, Mary Lou, Zoe, Liam, Rowan, and Mary C. Hetzer*

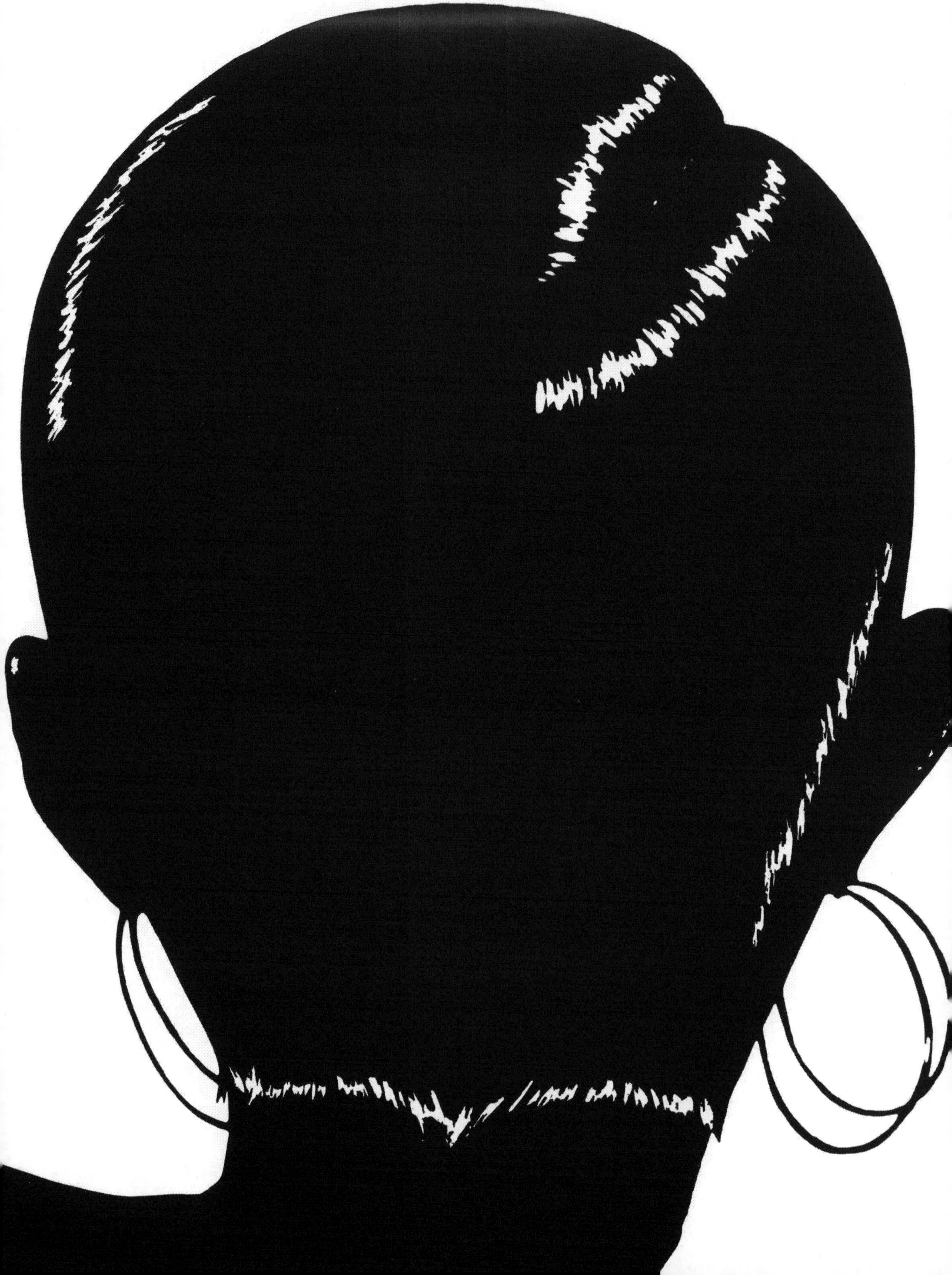

Made in United States
Orlando, FL
16 October 2022